THE BOOK OF INTRIGUING FACTS FOR SMART KIDS

A Book of Odd Facts for the Curious Mind

M PREFONTAINE

INTRODUCTION

I have no special talent. I am only passionately curious.
                                    Albert Einstein

When you think of facts you often think of the rather boring and mundane statistics of life. However not all facts are born equal. Some shed an intriguing and wonderful insight into the world around us.

This is a book for those who are eternally curious about life. A curiosity about life is the signature of the intelligent and enquiring mind. The searching out of the unusual, the counter intuitive and the downright bizarre are what feeds the search for knowledge.

No one is dumb who is curious. The people who don't ask questions remain clueless throughout their lives.
                                    Neil deGrasse Tyson

This book is a collection of facts from many different pursuits and genres which, in the mind of the author at least, are both odd and interesting. I hope you enjoy reading them as much as the author did in searching them out.

There is a liquid that you can breathe in called perfluorohexane. Animals can be submerged in a bath of oxygenated perfluorohexane without drowning.

The first vacuum cleaner was invented in 1901 by Henry Cecil Booth. It was horse drawn as it was so large.

At the end of the last ice age, about 6,000 years ago, the sea level had risen about 120 metres (390 feet).

The greenhouse gas carbon dioxide makes up just 0.04% of the Earth's atmosphere.

The sun loses about 5.5 million tonnes of mass every second. This is given off as energy.

Budimir Sobat holds the world record for holding his breath underwater at 24 minutes 37.36 seconds.

Shakespeare's Globe Theatre burnt down in 1613. During a performance of Henry VIII, they decided to use a real cannon for sound effects. The sparks set the thatched roof ablaze.

In our galaxy, which is called the Milky Way, there are estimated to be 400 million suns.

There are estimated to be 2 trillion galaxies. That is 2,000 million of them.

It has been estimated by Simon Driver, a professor at the International Centre for Radio Astronomy in Australia, that there are 70 thousand million, million, million, million stars. That is 7 followed by 22 zeros.

The world record distance covered in 24 hours walking backwards is 153.52km (95.4 miles). This was set by Anthony Thornton in Minneapolis on the 1st January 1989. His average speed was 3.975mph.

It is estimated that in adults 50 – 70 billion cells die per day. That is about 40 million per minute.

The moon is moving away from the earth at 3.78cm (1.48 inches) per year. This is measured by laser reflectors which were left on the moon during the Apollo mission.

When the moon was first formed, about 4.5 billion years ago, it is estimated that it orbited 14,000 miles away from the Earth, compared to 250,000 today. The moon being so close resulted in a day being only 5 hours long.

Krakatoa is a volcanic island between Java and Sumatra. In 1883 it exploded with the loudest explosion in recorded history. It was heard in Perth which is 3,110 km (1930 miles) away and the Tsunami travelled around the world three and a half times.

Switzerland is a landlocked country but still has a naval fleet of 10 ships which operate on lakes.

According to the World Health Organisation 627,000 people died of malaria in 2020.

St Paul's Cathedral, London, was burnt down in 1666 in the Great Fire London. It was rebuilt to the design of Sir Christopher Wren and was completed in 1716 at a cost of £1,095,556.

The largest known volcano is Olympus Mons at 72,000 feet. It is on Mars and was measured by the Mars Orbiter

The longest word in the Oxford English Dictionary has 45 letters and is pneumonoultramicroscopicsilicovolcanoconiosis. It is a lung disease that is formed through the inhalation of fine dust.

If a building is over 328 feet tall, which is about 40 or 50 stories, then it is considered a skyscraper. New York City has 257 skyscrapers.

There was a job called 'Groom of the Kings stool'. This job was to assist the king in excretion and hygiene. The position was finally abolished in 1901 when Edward VII came to the throne.

The largest spider is the Goliath Birdeater from South America. It can weigh 175g and has a leg span of up to 30cm (12 inches). It is big enough to cover a dinner plate.

There are 330 dimples on a golf ball.

If you place a wheat grain on a chess square, then two on the next, four on the next and so on you will end up with a pile of wheat which is 2,000 times the annual wheat production. This is 18,446,744,073,709,551,615.

The adult human body has 206 bones. A baby has 270 bones at birth, some of which fuse as the child develops.

The Great Wall of China is 21,196.18km (13,170 miles) long. This is over half the circumference of the earth.

Schiphol airport is used by over 70 million passengers per year. In 1571 it was the site of a major sea battle. The land was reclaimed from the sea by the Dutch.

The tallest tree in the world is a Sequoia called Hyperion in the Redwood National Park in California. It was measured at 380.3 feet.

The USA and Russia are about 3.8km (2.4 miles) apart at their closest point.

The tallest building in the world is the Burj Khalifa in Dubai, United Arab Emirates. The building was constructed in 2010 and is 828 metres high.

The sun has a circumference of 2,713,406 miles. The Earth's is 24,901 miles

The top speed of an ostrich is about 45 miles per hour.

Ada Lovelace was a mathematician and accepted as being the first computer programmer when she published an algorithm for Charles Babbage's calculating machine. She was born on the 10th December 1815.

Nikolai Tesla was a Serbian American inventor who demonstrated the first wireless radio message in St. Louis Missouri in 1893.

The first Oscar ceremony was in 1929 and lasted 15 minutes.

The earth can fit in the sun approximately 1,300,000 times.

Light travels at 299,792,458 kilometres per second

Dinosaurs were alive from about 243 to 231 million years ago to 65 million years ago, so they were about for 165 – 177 million years.

A light year is the distance that light travels in one year. It is 5,869,713,600,000 Miles.

The closest star to us, other than the sun, is Alpha Centauri which is 4.4 light years away. At the maximum speed of the space shuttle, which is 17,600 mph, this journey would take 165,000 years.

The oldest known tree is a Bristlecone Pine called Methuselah in the White Mountains of California. It was measured as being 4,845 years old.

There are 12 pints of blood in the body of an average sized man.

The universe was created in the Big Bang and there have been approximately 13.77 billion years since then.

The deepest ocean trench is the Marianna Trench in the Pacific. At its deepest it is 10,984 metres.

The first x-ray was taken (accidentally) on the 8th November 1895 by Wilhelm Conrad Rontgen while using a cathode ray generator.

The first census in the United States was completed on May 2nd, 1791. The final tally was that there were 3,929,214 people. The population is now over 329 million.

The sun is about 4,500 billion years old, which is some 9,300 million years after the universe was formed.

The longest scientifically measured Blue Whale is 98 feet.

There are estimated to be 200 billion brain cells in the human brain.

The first suns were believed to be formed 250 million years after the Big Bang.

There are estimated to be 1.5 billion Red Billed Queleas which is the most common bird in the world.

Surprisingly 10 Downing Street, the UK Prime Minister's residence, is reported to have 'approximately 100 rooms'.

The record number of children to a single mother, according to the Guinness Book of Records, is 69. The mother was Feodor Vassilyev (1707 – 1782) and had four sets of quadruplets, seven sets of triplets and 16 pairs of twins.

The lowest natural temperature ever recorded at ground level was at the Vostok Station in Antarctica when the temperature was recorded in July 1983 at -89.2 centigrade.

Bubble wrap was invented in 1957. It was unsuccessful as wallpaper and marketed as greenhouse insulation. IBM were the first to use it as a packaging material for the IBM1401 computer.

The Amazon rain forest is believed to be at least 55 million years old.

The number working for NASA on the Apollo space project, which landed men on the moon, was about 400,000 in total.

There is an average of 4 grams of iron in an average male body. The same as a 2.5 inch nail

Charles Babbage built a model of the first mechanical computer in 1822.

The record speed for solving a Rubik's Cube was set in 2016 by Yusheng Du from China at 3.47 seconds. A robot has been made which solved the puzzle in 0.38 seconds, though it did take the inventor, Erno Rubik, a month to solve when he invented it.

In 1816 Rene Laennec was the French doctor who invented the stethoscope. Before this invention doctors had to put their ear to the patient's chest to listen.

Some smaller mammoths survived on Wrangel Island, which is in the Arctic Ocean, till about 4,000 years ago.

The largest sequoia trees transport about 500 gallons up their trunks each day.

The smallest inhabited island in the world is called, appropriately, 'Just Room Enough Island' and is in the Thousand Islands Chain, belonging to New York. It extends to 3,300 square feet.

If you toss a coin 100 times the probability that you will end up with exactly 50 heads and 50 tails is 7.959%

Alaska was purchased by the US from Russia in 1867 for $7.2m.

The approximate speed the earth goes around the sun is 1100 miles per minute.

J.K. Rowling finished her first book 'Harry Potter and the Philosopher's Stone' in 1995. Rowling had 12 rejections before Bloomsbury eventually took her on and published the book. Much credit for this goes to the 8 year old daughter of the Bloomsbury Chairman who demanded the rest of the book after being shown the first chapter.

Artic Terns weigh about 4.5 ounces and migrates 22,000 miles annually according to the RSPB

An IQ of 150 is sometimes described as a 'genius level'. The chances of an individual having an IQ above 150 is 1 in 2,330. Given that the population of the UK is about 68.2 million that would mean that there 29,270 people in the UK with an IQ above 150.

Electricity was installed in the White House on the 14th September 1891. However, President Harrison and his wife were frightened of electricity and would never touch the light switches themselves, staff had to turn the lights on.

The largest individual tree is a Shaking Aspen called 'Pando' in the Fishlake National Forest in Colorado. It is in fact a clonal colony of 47,000 trees which have sprung from a single tree and covers 108 acres. It also weighs 6 million kilograms and is believed to be the heaviest organism.

On April 3rd 1973 the first handheld cellular phone call was made by Motorola engineer Martin Cooper from Sixth Avenue in New York. He called Joel Engel at his rival, Bell Industries, to inform him that Motorola had developed a functioning portable phone.

The last survivor of the Titanic to die was Millvina Dean who was 2 months old when she survived the sinking. She died on the 31st May 2009 aged 97.

Louis-Sebastien Lenormand made the first parachute jump with a contraption he invented when he jumped from the tower of Montpelier Observatory. The contraption was a 14 foot parachute with a rigid wooden frame and was used on December 26th, 1783.

Neutron stars are believed to be the fastest spinning objects in the universe, and some emit a pulse which allows this to be measured. The neutron star snappily named PSR J1748-2446sd is currently the fastest known spinning object. This star spins at an astonishing 716 revolutions per second. At its equator it is spinning at 24% of the speed of light.

According to worldatlas.com Holland has reclaimed about 2,700 square miles of land from the sea.

The average adult will inhale and exhale about 8 litres of air per minute. That is about 11,000 litres per day. Oxygen in the atmosphere is about 20% and in breath, when breathed out, 15%. Therefore 5% is consumed of 11,000 litres which means 550 litres of oxygen are consumed per day.

The moon is 27% the size of the earth.

168,000 cubic metres of water per minute go over Niagara Falls on average.

The Quetzalcoatl was one of the largest flying animals which lived around 100 million years ago. They are believed to have had a wingspan of up to 36 feet. The largest bird's wingspan today is the Wandering Albatross which has a wingspan of 8 to 11.5 feet.

Over 1 million earths could fit inside the sun if it were hollow.

An African elephant can reach speeds of 25 miles per hour.

The bamboo can grow up to 35 inches a day according to the Guinness Book of Records.

The Titanic was insured for £1,000,000, which cost the owners £7,500. The insurance companies were reported to have paid out $3,464,111.

On the 14th October 2012 Felix Baumgartner broke the record for freefall distance when he jumped from a helium balloon. He jumped from an altitude of 127,852 feet and fell 119,431 feet before landing in New Mexico. He reached a speed of 843mph.

The volume of water discharged by the Amazon River into the Atlantic Ocean is 219,000 cubic metres per second.

The latest numbers for people over 100 years old in the USA was for 2018 and revealed 93,927 centenarians. In 1950 it was 2,300.

The red supergiant star called UY Scuti is in the constellation Scutum and is one of the largest known stars. It is 5 billion times bigger than our sun.

It is not often that a cavalry attacks a naval fleet. However, this happened when a French Revolutionary Hussar regiment surrounded and captured 14 Dutch warships frozen in the sea 3 miles off Den Helder, Holland. The action happened on the 23rd January 1795. The Hussars managed to capture 14 naval ships, 850 guns and several merchant ships resulting in the conquest of the Netherlands by France.

Josephine Cochrane was the American inventor of the first commercially successful dishwasher. She said, "If nobody else is going to invent a dish washing machine, I'll do it myself". Josephine Cochrane got her patent on 28th December 1886.

There are 1860 steps to the top of the Empire State building.

The Temple of Artemis at Ephesus was one of the Seven Wonders of the Ancient World. It was destroyed when it was set on fire by Herostratus to immortalise his name. This act was said to have happened on the day Alexander the Great was born on the 21st July 356BC. Herostratus confessed to the crime and was executed. The authorities banned mention of his name orally and in writing to try and thwart the objective that Herostratus was trying to achieve, which clearly hasn't worked.

The Passenger Pigeon was a prolific North American bird. One flock in Ontario in 1866 was a mile wide and 300 miles long and took 14 hours to pass. However, they were hunted by settlers and were driven to extinction. The last Passenger Pigeon died in Cincinnati Zoo on the 1st September 1914.

In 1803 France sold Louisiana to the United States. The French, led by Napoleon, were paid $15 million for Louisiana.

The sun's diameter is 400.8 times bigger than the moon. By a remarkable coincidence the moon is 400 times closer to the earth than the sun which is why the moon covers the sun in a full eclipse.

The American Civil War ended in 1865 and Helen Viola Jackson was the last widow of a participant of the war to die. Remarkably she died on the 16th December 2020 which was 155 years after the end of the Civil War. During the Great Depression she helped veteran James Bolin with basic chores. As he was unable to pay her for the kindness, he married the 17 year old in 1936 so she would get a pension for life.

Caterpillars have 12 eyes, surprisingly.

Neutron stars are collapsed stars and the densest stars. According to NASA if you were able to collect a piece of a neutron star the size of a sugar cube it would weigh 1 billion tons on Earth, which is 1,000 million tons.

Vincent van Gogh struggled to sell his paintings and is only believed to have sold one during his lifetime. In May 1990, 100 years after his death, the painting, 'Portrait of Dr. Gachet', sold for $82.5 million.

The Antarctic Polar Desert is 5.5 million square miles and is the largest desert in the world.

The pH scale to test for alkalinity or acidity was invented by the Danish biochemist Soren Sorensen working in the Carlsberg beer laboratories in 1909.

There were 21,950,000 millionaires in the USA in 2021 according to the Global Wealth Report.

Nils Brohlin, working for Volvo cars, developed the three point seat belt which they gave away free to other car manufacturers for safety reasons in 1959.

On a news broadcast on the 18th April 1930 the BBC announced that 'there was no news today' before filling the time with piano music.

In the Hitchhiker's Guide to the Galaxy the number 42 is the answer to 'the meaning of life, the universe and everything'.

The oldest hotel in the world is Nishiyama Onsen Keiunkan, Japan, or the Hot Springs Hotel. It was founded in 705 A.D. by Fujiwara Mahito.

Sweden has a total of 267,570 islands according to a 2013 statistical report. Less than 1,000 are inhabited and they form about 3% of the land area of Sweden.

According to the Guinness Book of Records Walter Arnold was the first person to be charged with speeding. He was spotted on the 28th January 1896 going four times the limit in his Benz through the village of Paddock Wood. He was going at the breakneck speed of 8 mph.

The peculiar traditional hat a chef wears is called a 'toque' and dates back to the 16th Century. It has 100 folds, which are said to represent the number of ways an egg can be cooked.

Art competitions used to be held as part of the Olympics. Medals were awarded in five categories (architecture, music, literature, painting, and sculpture). The last Olympic art competition was held in 1948.

The average pencil holds enough graphite to draw a line 35 miles long, or to write 45,000 words.

The longest recorded flight of a chicken is 13 seconds.

On the 28th June 2009 Stephen Hawking, the famous physicist, carried out an experiment in which threw a party for space travellers. He advertised the party after it happened on the basis that someone from the future would be able to go back in time and attend. Unfortunately, no one attended.

A skydiver will reach their terminal velocity of about 195 km/h (122 mph) after about 10 seconds. They won't increase in speed after this because gravity and the air resistance from falling will have equal magnitude and cancel each other out.

Polio was a widespread and crippling disease. In 1977 the World Health Organisation estimated that there were 254,000 living in the USA paralysed by polio. Jonas Salk was an American virologist who invented a vaccine for the disease. He decided not to patent it so that it was free to the world. The vaccine came into use in 1955.

When the dinosaurs were alive there were still volcanos on the moon.

Human hair can grow at up to 6 inches per year.

According to the Guinness Book of Records the biggest gap between the birth of twins is 90 days born in 1996 in Baltimore, Maryland.

A 'Dancing Plague' started in Strasbourg in July 1518 where up to 400 people danced uncontrollably and apparently unwillingly for days on end, beyond the point of injury. The mania disappeared as mysteriously as it had begun after about two months.

A hummingbird heart can reach 12,600 beats per minute. A human heartbeat is normally between 60 and 100 beats per minute.

Europe and the US are physically moving away from each other due to something called continental drift. They are moving apart at an average of 1 inch per year.

The pygmy three toed sloth is the slowest mammal in the world. It can manage about 260 yards per hour.

The unfortunate Charles Osborne, following an accident at work, began hiccupping in 1922 at the age of 29 and continued for 68 years. They stopped for the last year of his life before he died in 1991 aged 97.

The Average NFL game lasts 3 hours and 12 minutes. According to an analysis by the Wall St Journal the ball is in play for just 11 minutes. The average game has over 100 adverts.

In a room of 35 people the probability that two of these people will have the same birthday is 85%.

In a game of chess if each player has made three moves the pieces could be in over 9 million different positions.

According to the Bosley hair transplant company there are 250 hairs in an average eyebrow.

If you have $0.01 saved up and doubled it every day you would be a millionaire in 27 days.

You need 23 people for a greater than 50% probability of two of the people having the same birthday.

As we know the earth is spinning, but if you are standing on the equator, you are spinning faster than if you are standing at the poles. The equator is 24,901 miles long and has one full revolution per 24 hours. You would be spinning at a speed of 1,037mph on the equator.

On the 26th January 1972 Vesna Vulovic was a flight attendant on a flight from Stockholm to Belgrade. A bomb was aboard the plane, and it exploded, and the plane broke apart. Vulovic was the only survivor and holds the record for surviving the biggest fall without a parachute. She fell from 33,330 feet and suffered severe injuries but is reported to have made an almost complete physical recovery.

Death Valley's Badwater Basin is the lowest point in North America. It is 86 metres below sea level.

Dyrehavsbakken in Denmark is the world's oldest operating amusement park. It opened in 1583 and was centred around a natural spring which was believed to have curative properties.

According to the War Graves Commission a total of 863 British and Commonwealth soldiers died on the last day of World War 1, November 11th, 1918.

The world's oldest known paved road is six and a half feet wide and covered seven and a half miles connecting quarries south of Cairo. The road is over 4,600 years old.

The King's School in Canterbury claims to be the oldest existing school in the world. It was founded in 597 AD, a century after the fall of the Roman Empire.

Initially cocaine was an ingredient of Coca Cola. It was common in medicines at the time and was thought to be relatively harmless. It was eliminated from the drink in 1929.

Vincenzo Perrugia committed what has been called the art theft of the century when he stole the Mona Lisa from the Louvre. He stole the painting on the 21st August 1911. It was returned to the Louvre in 1913.

Despite finishing bottom of his class at West Point General Custer with a record number of 726 demerit points George Custer became, in 1863, one of the youngest US Generals when he was 23 years old. He died at the Battle of the Little Bighorn.

Henry VII who defeated Richard III at the Battle of Bosworth on the 24th August 1485 was the last English king to gain the crown on the battlefield.

The Circus Maximus was originally laid out in the 6th Century BC and was used by the Romans for chariot racing. It could hold 150,000 spectators.

Surprisingly, Rio de Janeiro was the capital of Portugal for a period despite being 4,800 miles away. It became the capital of Portugal on March 7th, 1808, when the United

Kingdom of Portugal, Brazil and the Algarve was created. This was necessitated as Napoleonic forces had invaded Lisbon in December 1807. Rio ceased to be the capital in 1821.

Voyager 1 was launched in 1977 and is the fastest man made object. It has taken photos of various planets including the famous 'pale blue dot photo' of earth. Voyager 1 is travelling at 523.6 million kilometres a year.

HMS Birkenhead was a British troopship which sank after hitting a reef near South Africa on the 25th February 1852. Many lifeboats could not be used, and soldiers famously stood aside which gave rise to the 'women and children first' protocol.

According to the University of Kentucky a male mosquito is capable of up to 600 wingbeats per second.

Of men who flew a sortie for the RAF Bomber Command in World War II 56% were killed. This is a total of 55,573 airmen who died.

The rather creepy estimate is that there is an average of 50 million bacteria per square inch of human skin.

Outer space is -270.42 centigrade. Given that absolute zero is -273.15 outer space is distinctly chilly.

The odds of tossing 20 heads in a row is 1 in 1,048,576 or about 1 in a million.

Stanislaw Kowalski, from Poland, is the world's oldest athlete. At 105 years old he ran 100 metres in 34.50 seconds.

Usain Bolt holds the world record for the fastest 100 metres in 9.58 seconds. If Usain was unwise enough to jump off a 100 metre building it would take him 4.52 seconds to hit the floor.

A 'parsec' is 3.26 light years. It is used to measure large distances beyond our solar system.

According to the United Nations there are estimated to be 573,000 centenarians in 2021.

There are 600 muscles in the human body but over 40,000 muscles in an elephant's trunk.

Eric 'Winkle' Brown flew more different types of aircraft than anyone else in history. He flew 487 in total.

The last bare knuckle heavyweight championship boxing contest was in 1889 when John L Sullivan defeated Jake Kilrain in the 75th round. Kilrain's second threw in the sponge to concede defeat.

The human population is growing by about 215,000 per day.

The World Health Organisation estimate that 1,300,000 die annually in traffic accidents.

The shortest war in recorded history was the Anglo-Zanzibar war of 1896. It happened on the 27th August 1897 and lasted for between 38 and 45 minutes. The issue was a dispute about a new Sultan. The British issued an ultimatum for 9.00am. There was then a skirmish which involved sinking the Zanzibari royal yacht. The prospective Sultan then fled to the German Embassy.

The average full stop would hold about 2 million hydrogen atoms.

There are one billion nanoseconds in a second.

Worker ants, assuming ideal conditions, can live up to 15 years.

The American Civil War saw more American casualties than the two World Wars, the Vietnam War and the Korean War put together. According to the American Battlefield Trust there were an estimated 620,000 dead. This was from a population of about 31.4 million at the time.

According to the National Geographic 2,000 people are killed by lightening every year.

Janet Horne was the last witch to be executed in the UK in 1727.

George Eyser was a German-American gymnast who competed in the 1904 St. Louis Olympics despite having a wooden leg. He won 6 medals, including 3 gold medals, despite losing his leg in a train accident. One of the gold medals was the vault without the aid of a springboard in those days.

Yale University began to accept women in 1969.

According to the LA Times at least 30 million Chinese live in caves.

The Bay of Fundy, in Canada, has the biggest tidal range in the world at 38 feet.

The Halifax explosion happened on the 6th December 1917 and 1,782 people were confirmed killed. It happened in Halifax, Nova Scotia Canada. It was the result of the collision of two ships with one fully laden with high explosives and the other with coal. The explosion was the largest man made explosion till that time.

Cornelis Drebbel, a Dutch engineer and inventor, built the first navigable submarine while working for the Royal Navy. He built it in 1620 and even took King James on a test dive under the Thames.

According to NASA an object which weighed 1,000kg at the South Pole would weigh 996.5kg at the equator. This 3.5kg loss is due to the centrifugal forces of the earth.

The Dodo, most famous for being extinct, was first mentioned by Dutch sailors in 1598, but the last recorded sighting was in 1662.

The cost of the Model T Ford car was $850 when it was launched in 1908, with the price falling every year after that. It is regarded as the first affordable motor car.

Growing large pumpkins is an extremely competitive area. The heaviest so far was grown by Belgian Mathias Willemijns and was authenticated on October 9th 2016. The pumpkin weighed 2,634.6 pounds.

Zefram Cochrane, according to Star Trek at least, made (will make?) Earth's first Warp Drive flight on April 5th 2063.

Private Teuro Nakamura was a Japanese soldier in World War 2. He was discovered by the Indonesian Air Force on the island of Morotai unaware that World War 2 had ended on December 18th, 1974. This was 29 years 3 months and 16 days after the Japanese surrender.

The Rosetta Stone is a stone text of a decree that was issued in Egypt and is written in three languages which allowed for the deciphering of Egyptian hieroglyphics. The Rosetta Stone's decree was written around 196 BC.

Ulaan – Baatar is the capital of Mongolia and the coldest capital in the world. The average temperature is a chilly - 0.4 centigrade.

Mach 1, which is the speed of sound, is approximately 761 miles per hour.

Mercury becomes a solid at -38.83 centigrade.

The Hawaiian alphabet has 12 letters.

The Earth was formed 4.54 million years ago

The first telephone book was produced for New Haven, Connecticut, in February 1878. It had 50 names and no numbers. People rang the operator to be connected.

Polyethylene terephthalate is a plastic that is commonly used for plastic bottles. It takes 450 years to fully decompose.

The Greek national anthem is 'Anthem to Liberty' and was written in 1823 and extends to 158 verses.

There are at least 70 pieces of wood in a violin.

According to the Guinness Book of Records Sean Shannon is the fastest talker. He can speak 655 words per minute.

The Rosetta Stone was discovered on the 15th July 1799 by Napoleon's troops who were digging in a couple of miles from the Egyptian port of Rosetta. When the British defeated the French the Rosetta Stone was taken to London and has been in the British Museum since 1802.

There are over 200 viruses that are known to cause the common cold.

Stonehenge was built in various phases but was begun in 3000 – 2920 BC.

Salt is 3.5% of the oceans. The Dead Sea is 34% salt.

If you dropped an object from a height of 100 metres it would be doing 99 mph as it hit the ground.

There are about 50 quintillion atoms in a grain of sand. A quintillion is 1 followed by 18 zeros.

The Dunning-Kruger effect is a hypothetical bias that people with low ability at a task overestimate their ability. The social psychologist's inspiration for this theory came from the case of McArthur Wheeler who robbed two banks in 1995 having covered his face with lemon juice, believing this made him invisible.

The Oxford English Dictionary gives quarterly updates where they add new words to the dictionary which have become popular. In June 2021 they added 676 new words. These included 'staycation' and 'social distance'.

The loudest animal on earth is the Sperm Whale and has been measured at 230 decibels. Blue Whales are a mere 188 decibels.

The word 'hexakosioihexekontahexaphobia' is the irrational fear of the number 666

Giraffes have seven bones in their necks which is the same as humans.

The original Granny Smith apple was grown from a chance seedling by Maria Ann Smith in Eastwood, New South Wales, Australia. All Granny Smith's today are clones of the original tree which was first identified in 1838.

According to the Guinness Book of Records Captain Oguri Jukichi was adrift for 484 days after his ship was damaged in a storm off the Japanese coast in 1813. He was finally rescued off California on the 24th March 1815.

A Quahog Clam which was dredged up off Iceland is the longest lived recorded animal. The age of the clam was determined by counting the growth rings and was 507 years old.

Solo Synchronised Swimming was a sport that was competed for in the Olympics. The last Olympic Solo Synchronised Swimming event was in the Olympics of 1992 in Barcelona.

Lincoln Cathedral was the tallest building in the world from the completion of its spire in 1311 till 1548 when an earthquake collapsed the spire.

The Mousetrap, by Agatha Christie, is the longest running theatrical production. It had its world premiere at the Theatre Royal, Nottingham, on the 6th October 1952.

Sound takes 4.7 seconds to travel a mile. You can tell the approximate distance of lightening from you by counting the seconds.

Canada's coastline is approximately 151,019 miles long.

In Italy the number 17 is held superstitiously to be bad luck.

The River Thames has frozen over during several very cold periods and 'Frost Fairs' have been held on the Thames. The last Frost Fair on the Thames began on the 1st February 1814 and lasted 4 days. An elephant was led across the Thames below Blackfriars Bridge.

The novella, Futility, was written by Morgan Robertson. It is about a fictional British Ocean Liner, The Titan, which sinks in the North Atlantic after hitting an iceberg. It was published in 1898, which was 14 years before the Titanic foundered on its maiden voyage.

Dark Energy is a theoretical repulsive force in physics that repels gravity. According to NASA 68% of the universe is Dark Energy. Dark Matter makes up 27% of the rest which leaves 5% for everything else we have ever seen. No, I do not understand it either but that is the current thinking.

Former president George W Bush was a cheerleader at Yale University.

There were 2,927 RAF flyers involved in the Battle of Britain, from many nationalities, and 510 were killed.

The French physicist, mathematician and inventor Blaise Pascal created the first roulette wheel in 1655. He was not trying to create a casino game but a perpetual motion machine

The Bootlace Worm is the longest animal. In 1864 a specimen was washed ashore at St Andrew's which measured 180 feet long.

There are 2,618 toilets in Wembley Stadium.

A tsunami can travel at about 500 mph over open ocean. They are shallow and very long waves in the ocean but slow up in shallow water and the wave builds to create the destructive tsunami wave.

The Canada and USA border is the longest international border in the world. The border is 5,525 miles long.

The Cosmic Year is the amount of time it takes for our sun to revolve around our galaxy. The Sun's Cosmic Year is approximately 230 million years.

Octopuses and squids have beaks. The beak is made of keratin which is the same material as a bird's beak, and our fingernails are made of.

In 2007, Scotland spent £125,000 devising and installing a new national slogan. The winning entry was: "Welcome to Scotland".

Until 2016, the "Happy Birthday" song was not for public use. Meaning, prior to 2016, the song was copyrighted, and you had to pay a license to use it. The song is attributed to American sisters Patty and Mildred Hill who wrote it in 1893. Warner/Chappell Music claimed copyright for any commercial use and collected revenue of about $2 million per year. In 2015 the copyright was declared invalid.

More tornadoes occur in the United Kingdom per square mile than any other country in the world. They are generally small but one in Birmingham in 2005 injured 19 people and caused £40 million of damage.

God is the only Simpsons character who has five fingers. All the rest of the characters only have four.

Despite having much fantastic wildlife, the national animal of Scotland is a unicorn. It was first used on the Scottish royal coat of arms in the 12th Century.

In 1999, PayPal was voted as one of the top ten worst business ideas. Twenty three years later the company is worth over $50 billion.

Every 10 years, the human skeleton repairs and renews itself. Essentially, you have different bones now than you did 10 years ago.

The water dropwort is a highly poisonous plant. If it kills you, it can cause you to smile after you die. This is caused by the hemlock water dropwort and is called a sardonic grin.

The insurance company that backed the big pay-outs for "Who Wants to Be a Millionaire" sued the American version of the show saying the show had questions so basic it was easy to win.

Tyromancy is the practice of predicting the future by using cheese. Such features as mould, smell and how cheese melts allow followers to make various predictions of the future.

You might think that the Battle of Hastings in 1066 took place at Hastings, but no. It took place about 7 miles away from Hastings at a place confusingly called 'Battle'.

The smallest thing ever photographed is the shadow of an atom of the element ytterbium by a team from the University of Australia. The object is 0.4 millionths of a millimetre.

Despite Mercury being the closest planet to the Sun, Venus is the warmest planet. This is because Venus, unlike Mercury, has an atmosphere and it mostly consists of carbon dioxide. This has created a runaway greenhouse effect.

Pope Francis used to be a nightclub bouncer. As a student in his birthplace Buenos Aires, he worked as a nightclub bouncer to support himself.

In 1942, a 12-year-old lied about his age to join the Navy. He became a decorated war hero at age 13 but was thrown out of the Navy after his mum found out.

In 2018 Nebraska released a new state slogan *Nebraska. Honestly, it's not for everyone". The Tourism Director pointed out that Nebraska was the state least likely to be visited by tourists, and he said, "We had to shake people up".

You can get an insurance policy against alien abduction. Around 50,000 policies have been sold, mainly to residents of the U.S. and UK. Disappointingly there have been no reports of any successful claims.

At the 1968 Mexico Olympics on the 18th October Bob Beamon jumped 29 feet 2.5 inches to win the gold medal. This was over 21 inches further than anyone had jumped before. No one had jumped 28 feet let alone 29 feet prior.

President Ulysses S. Grant was arrested while in office. He was charged, booked, and released for speeding on a horse-drawn carriage in Washington. He paid the fine of $20.

The paint on the Eiffel Tower weighs about 60 tonnes, the same as ten elephants. It gets repainted every seven years without being closed to the public.

Humans lose between 30 – 40,000 skin cells every hour, which is nearly 1 million per day.

Queen Elizabeth saved up post-war clothing ration coupons to pay for the material for her wedding dress in 1947.

The longest word that can be spelled without repeating a letter is subdermatoglyphic. It refers to patterns under the skin that determine fingerprints.

If you point your car keys to your head, it increases the remote's signal range. This works by using your brain to act as a radio transmitter and can extend the remotes range by a few car lengths.

During the 1908 Olympics in London, the Russians showed up 12 days late since they were using the Julian calendar instead of the Gregorian calendar.

Rebecca Felton was the first woman to ever serve for the United States Senate in 1922. However, she only served for one day. She was also the last member of congress to own a slave.

A collective group of lemurs is called a conspiracy.

The Ethiopian calendar is 7.5 years behind the Gregorian calendar since it has 13 months.

The last 'Timeless Test cricket match' played in 1939 against South Africa lasted over 12 days. It was designed to continue playing to ensure a result but ended as a draw. The English team had to leave, despite being in sight of victory, as they would have missed their boat home.

Thomas Edison invented an electric pen in 1876 and it was later adapted to become the first electric tattoo needle in 1891.

In 2012, a missing woman on vacation in Iceland was found when it was discovered that she was in the search party, and she realised they were looking for her.

At least 330 people worldwide have died taking selfies, mostly from falls.

30 of the first 31 popes were murdered.

When the Titanic sank in 1912, there were 3 dogs that survived. They had all been traveling with their owners in the First Class cabins.

Enceladus, one of Saturn's smaller moons, reflects 90% of the sunlight, making it more reflective than snow.

Papua New Guinea has 832 living languages and over 200 dialects.

There are 398 species of parrots. Only one can't fly - the Kakapo parrot from New Zealand.

The front paws of a cat are different from the back paws. They have five toes on the front but only four on the back.

Aggressive sitting is a sport which originated in Berlin. You can purchase a special stool, which is central for this sport, for around 70 dollars.

Berries are simple fruits having a seed and fleshy pulp produced by one flower. This means that pineapples, bananas, watermelon, pumpkins, and avocados are berries.

Mercury and Venus are the only two planets in our solar system that do not have any moons because they are too close to the sun.

Ed Sheeran has a ketchup bottle tattooed on his left arm.

Despite the name only 45% of the London Underground is underground.

In 2013, a plant was grafted that grew tomatoes above ground, and potatoes underground. It is called the TomTato.

"Jayus", is a useful Indonesian word that means "A joke told so bad it is funny".

Dolly Parton lost in a Dolly Parton look-alike contest to a man.

It takes longer to drown in saltwater than in freshwater. Partly because of this, around 90% of drownings occur in freshwater

Boanthropy is a psychological disorder that makes people believe they are a cow.

In 1986, a soviet Aeroflot pilot bet the co-pilot he could land the plane blind. 70 of the 94 passengers on board were killed in the crash.

In 1911, Bobby Leach was the 2nd person to go over Niagara Falls in a barrel. He died 15 years later from slipping on an orange peel and getting gangrene.

In 1325 the War of the Bucket was fought between two Italian city states. The bucket was taken as a trophy and 2,000 died.

There are somewhere between 100,000 and 150,000 hairs on your head, and each of them grows about a half-inch per month. In total, your hair grows 1.1 inches in a minute.

It has been shown that the average person blinks 15-20 times every minute. This means that humans spend about 10 percent of their time awake with their eyes closed.

Each heartbeat pumps about 2.4 ounces of blood and sends it throughout your body. If you have a resting heart rate of 80 beats per minute, your heart pumps 1.5 gallons of blood every 60 seconds.

In 1985 in New Orleans a party was held for Lifeguards to celebrate that no one had died at any of the City's pools. Unfortunately, despite over 100 lifeguards being in attendance, one person died by drowning.

The world's smallest mammal is a Bumblebee Bat, from Myanmar and Thailand. They are 1 to 1.3 inches long

The Great Pyramid of Giza has eight sides, rather than four. This is because the sides are concave.

In 1992, a shipping crate containing 28,800 rubber duck went overboard on the way to the USA from China. They are still being washed up around the world.

So far, two diseases have successfully been eradicated: smallpox and rinderpest. The last case of smallpox was in 1977, and the last of rinderpest was in 2001.

There are records of ant queens living for up to 30 years, though 10 years is more typical.

There were plans by the Mayor of Montreal and Charles de Gaulle to ship the Eiffel Tower to Montreal for the 1976 Olympics.

In 1923 a jockey called Frank Hayes suffered a fatal heart attack during a race. Despite being dead in the saddle his horse, Sweet Kiss, still won the race.

A red blood cell takes only about 20 seconds to make a complete circuit through your body.

The first photograph ever shot in 1826, 'View from the window at Le Gras', took 8 hours of exposure.

The Vatican City is second on the list of per capita wine consuming countries. They consume 56.2 litres per year.

Nicholas Cage bought a pet octopus for £110,000.

No piece of A4 paper can be folded in half more than 7 times.

In 2005, a fortune cookie company called Wonton Food Inc. correctly foretold the lottery numbers. This resulted in 110 winners winning up to $500,000 each. No fraud was involved, and they were paid.

A Portuguese Man of War is not a jellyfish. It is a siphonophore which is a colony of thousands of individual animals called "zooids"

The dates from 5th October 1582 to 15th October 1582 don't exist due to the change from Julian calendar to Gregorian calendar in most of Europe.

Death by GPS refers to the death of people attributable, in part, to following GPS directions or GPS maps. There have been several such deaths in California.

In 1993, Toronto lawyer Garry Hoy was doing his favorite trick of hurling himself at his office's windows to show their strength. But this time the glass came out of the frame, and he fell to his death.

James Heselden OBE was a British entrepreneur who bought Segway Inc., maker of the Segway personal transport system. He died in 2010 from injuries apparently sustained falling from a cliff while riding his own product.

Green Eggs and Ham was written by Dr Seuss and started as a bet. Dr. Seuss bet with his editor that he could not create a book using fewer than 50 different words. It has sold over 8 million copies.

Every 100 years, the moon adds approximately 1.4 milliseconds to a day. When dinosaurs were alive, days were 23 hours long, according to NASA.

Giant squids have the largest eyes of any animal on Earth. They are 11 inches across.

Coca-Cola was first served in 1886 and sold as patent medicine. At that time, only 9 colas were served on an average day. Today, over 10,000 Coca-Cola soft drinks are consumed every second.

John Hopkins estimates that 9.5% of all deaths in the USA are due to medical error.

It takes 20 seconds for a child to drown according to US Army Corps of Engineers (USACE).

By examining their data, Wal-Mart determined that people stock up the most on strawberry Pop-Tarts and beer before a hurricane.

The town of Monowi in Nebraska has a population of one. The only resident is a woman who is the Mayor, Bartender, and Librarian.

The 2020 census listed 2 residents in Monowi. After a complaint the Census Bureau admitted that an individual from a neighbouring area had been added to protect the identity of the individual.

The Roman – Persian wars are the longest in history, lasting over 720 years. They began in 92 BC and ended in 628 AD.

Standing around burns calories. On average, a 150-pound person burns 114 calories per hour while standing and doing nothing.

Facebook created two AI chatbots, named Alice and Bob, to talk to each other. They started communicating in a language they made for themselves.

During WWII, the U.S. naval destroyer O'Bannon won a battle against a Japanese submarine by throwing potatoes at them. The Japanese thought they were grenades.

The quietest room in the world is at the Orfield Laboratories in Minnesota and the sound is measured in negative decibels. The longest that anybody has been able to bear it is 45 minutes.

A bolt of lightning can reach 50-70,000 degrees Fahrenheit.

Lightning comes in different colours.

A French general, Marquis de Lafayette, gave President John Quincy Adams a pet alligator. Adams kept it in a White House bathtub and enjoyed showing it off.

Underneath the streets of Beijing, there are between 100,000 and 1 million people who live in nuclear bunkers.

Thomas Midgley (1889 – 1944), was an American inventor. His two most famous inventions are both now banned because they are dangerous for the world environment: the use of lead in petrol (gasoline) and the use of chlorofluorocarbons (CFCs) in refrigerators. He devised an elaborate system of ropes and pulleys to lift himself out of bed. In 1944, he became entangled in the device and died of strangulation.

The Earth is the densest planet in the solar system.

Research at Newcastle University found that feeding coriander and turmeric, curry spices, to a sheep reduces the amount of methane in its farts by up to 40%.

Despite being landlocked, Mongolia has a navy consisting of seven men and one vessel. The "Sukhbaatar III" is stationed on Lake Khövsgöl.

Oranges aren't naturally occurring fruits. Oranges are a hybrid of tangerines and pomelos, also known as "Chinese grapefruit," and they were originally green.

A 2016 study found that a 154-pound man has about 38 trillion bacteria in his body, which is roughly the same as the amount of human cells.

28 is the number of times that cycling champion Miguel Indurain's record-setting heart would beat each minute while at rest.

A single neuron can send as many as 1,000 nerve impulses every second (or 60,000 per minute). A healthy human brain has about 200 billion neurons. That adds up to 12,000,000,000,000,000 signals being sent throughout your brain.

Some insects and small birds see the world in slow motion. They process information so quickly that they perceive time as though it was in slow motion.

The most expensive domain name ever sold was cars.com for $872.3 million.

Apart from a few organs, caterpillars liquefy almost completely while undergoing metamorphosis.

Jellyfish are considered biologically immortal. They don't age and will never die unless they are killed.

One calorie from food equals 4,200 joules of energy, so a person who consumes 2,000 calories a day uses about 5,832 joules per minute. That's enough to power a bright light bulb with only your body.

One species of jellyfish, Turritopsis nutricula, is considered biologically immortal as it can—and does—revert to its immature state even after reaching sexual maturity.

During a conversation each speaker's "turn" averages 2 seconds, and the pause in between is only 200 milliseconds. That figure is nearly universal.

In Switzerland, it is illegal to own just one guinea pig. This is because guinea pigs are social animals and would be lonely.

Polar bear liver is highly toxic due to it storing vitamin A to counter reduced winter sunlight. 30 to 90 grams of polar bear liver is enough to kill a human being.

There is a Guinness world record for the longest amount of time needed to create an official government – it is held by Belgium. The record for the longest period without a government. It was 541 days after the election in 2010.

In the UK in 1994 a judge ordered a retrial of a murder case after the jury used a Ouija board to try and contact one of the murder victims.

Coconuts can crack open when they're in the freezer.

According to scientists, the weight of the average cumulus cloud is about 500 tonnes.

The Fiat factory in Turin, Italy, had an entire racetrack on the roof.

Edvard Munch's famous painting "The Scream" was painted on cardboard

An ant can't die from falling.

40 million years ago there were penguins which were 6 feet tall and weighed 170 pounds.

Chrysomallon squamiferum is a species of snail that lives near deep-sea hydrothermalvents. It has an iron shell.

The earliest undisputed evidence of life on earth is 3.5 billion years old.

M&Ms were inspired by a method used to allow soldiers in the Spanish Civil War (1936–1939) to carry chocolate in warm climates without it melting.

The first ever 3D film was 'The Power of Love' and released in 1922.

Scientist Professor Randy Lewis genetically modified goats to spin spider silk from their udders at a farm in Utah.

Broccoli only came about after years and years of selective breeding between wild cabbage plants which started around the 6th century BC.

Peanuts, walnuts, almonds, cashews and pistachios aren't nuts. They're classed as seeds, because a nut is defined as "a hard-shelled dry fruit or seed with a separable rind or shell and interior kernel".

Most perfume is made using ambergris, which is Sperm Whale sick.

We have roughly 30 trillion cells in our bodies, and red blood cells account for about 80% of these.

Three types of Australian birds deliberately spread wildfires. Black kites, whistling kites and brown falcons all purposefully aid the spread of wildfires by dropping flaming sticks so the fire will force out their prey.

In 2009 A French and British stealth nuclear submarine collided into each other by accident

A 1783 volcanic eruption killed 20% of Iceland's population because of famine.

When your mother was born, she was already carrying the egg that would eventually become you.

Since 1962 Jousting is the official sport of the state of Maryland.

"Rain of fish" is an annual weather event in which hundreds of fish rain from the sky onto the Honduran city of Yoro.

A mouse can fit through a hole the size of about 6 – 7 mm which is the diameter of a normal pen.

In 30 minutes, the human body gives off enough heat to bring a gallon of water to a boil.

Around 55 million people alive right now will be dead within 12 months.

The word 'Arctic' means bear and Antarctic 'Opposite the Bears'.

In the early 1900s, there was a pod of killer whales which the indigenous Yuin people used to hunt down other whales in Australia. They would be rewarded with the fins and tongues of the captured whales. This was known as "The Law of Tongue".

Manatees can get frostbite in cold weather. Their fat does not insulate them from the cold.

You are taller in the morning than in the evening.

The 'Great Smog of London' in 1952 lasted 5 days and is estimated to have killed 10-12,000 people.

There are more than 70 fungi that glow in the dark to attract insects.

When you remember a past event, you are remembering the last time you remembered it, not the event itself.

Movie trailers were originally shown after the movie, which is why they're called "trailers". This proved ineffective as the audience didn't bother to stay to watch them, so they changed it.

Your skin is an organ.

The gene that gives extra fingers or toes is a dominant one. This means that if you get one of these genes from your parents you will have the condition.

A Knocker-Upper woke people up in the morning shooting peas on the window. They earned about 6 pence (2.5p) per week.

If your body gets severely low on vitamin C, your old scars will open back up, even surgical scars. It's because even though they seem dormant and healed they are actually constantly regenerating, which requires vitamin C.

In 1363, during the Hundred Years War, there was a mandate that all Englishmen had to practice with their longbow every Sunday.

During the 1800s British noblemen in India would use so called 'Jellyboys' (local boys smeared in jam) to walk beside them attracting all the bugs, flies and mosquitoes.

A species of alpine bee has been recorded at heights over 30,000 feet above sea.

About 20% of all mammal species on Earth are bats. There are about 1400 species of bat.

On statues, a horse's legs tell you how the statue figure died. If a horse has both its front legs in the air, then the person died in battle. If the horse has one of its front legs in the air, they died of wounds received from a battle. And if the horse has both its front legs on the ground then the person died of natural causes.

For every pound of fat gained, you add seven miles of new blood vessels.

A Blue Whale's heart is the size of a VW Beetle and large enough that you could swim through its arteries.

Goats have rectangular pupils.

There are more cars than people in Los Angeles. There are about 4 million inhabitants and 6 million vehicles.

The best estimate is that 205,000 tonnes of gold has ever been mined. This would result in a cube of 22 metres on each side if collected.

The world's longest musical piece lasts 639 years. An organ in St. Burchardi church in Halberstadt in 2001 began a performance that is due to end in 2640. The next note will be played on February 5, 2024.

Kurt Godel was a mathematician and was so paranoid of being poisoned that he would only eat his wife's cooking. When she became hospitalised, he starved to death.

Muscle tissue is three times more efficient at burning calories than fat. More muscles will mean more calories will be burned.

Scientists discovered sharks that are living in an active underwater volcano off the Solomon Islands. Divers cannot investigate as it is too dangerous.

There is 'snow' on mountains of Venus. The 'snow' that has been found is made from galena and bismuthinite which are metals.

If you cut a starfish, it won't bleed. They don't have any blood. Rather, they circulate nutrients by using seawater in their vascular system.

In 2005, Connecticut was accidentally issued an Emergency Alert to evacuate the entire state. Only about 1% of the people tried to leave.

Your face is a crumple zone. If you fall on your face, it helps you avoid brain damage by absorbing the shock.

The World Chess Champion G. Kasparov described Hungarian female chess player Polgár as a "circus puppet" and said that women chess players should stick to having children. In September 2002, in the Russia versus the Rest of the World Match, Polgár duly defeated Garry Kasparov

The collective noun for gnus is 'an implausibility of gnus'.

People with chromesthesia "see" color in sounds.

Fingers don't have muscles. They have tendons which are moved by the muscles of the forearm

The bananas you buy don't reproduce by seeds any more.

Nauru is the only country in the world without an official capital city.

Mexican law explicitly declares that there is no penalty for prison escape

Platypuses have stingers on their hind feet which can inject painful venom.

Psychology is the brain trying to comprehend itself.

It is claimed that more than 2,500 left-handed people are killed every year from using equipment meant for right-handed people.

Starfish can regenerate. A single arm can regenerate a whole body.

There's a basketball court above the Supreme Court. It's known as the Highest Court in the Land.

There is a garbage swirl in the Pacific Ocean, known as the Great Pacific Garbage Patch, which is the size of Texas.

Horses are nasal breathers and cannot breathe through their mouths.

A blue whale's tongue weighs as much as a female elephant.

A "jiffy" is an actual unit of time. A jiffy is typically considered to be 0.01 seconds, or 10 milliseconds.

Fleas can jump up to 100 times their body length.

Tsutomu Yamaguchi was a Japanese marine engineer and survived both the Hiroshima and Nagasaki atomic bombings and lived to be 93.

Babies don't have bony kneecaps.

The magnetic North Pole is moving. It is different to the actual North Pole and is in northern Canada. It moves about 10 kilometres a year.

A 2015 study published in the Journal of the American Planning Association determined that 14 percent of Los Angeles incorporated land is devoted to parking.

If you close your eyes in a completely dark room. When you open them, the color you see is called eigengrau. It's the shade of dark grey which people see when there's no light.

You can download the whole of Wikipedia and keep it on a USB drive.

Four-year-old girls ask an average of 390 questions per day. Nine-year-old boys ask an average of 144 questions per day.

Every year, an average of 69 Americans are killed by lawnmowers.

Mars is populated entirely by robots.

When you look "up" at the sky, what you are doing is looking down into the apparently infinite abyss of space. It is only gravity that is holding you to the planet's surface.

 If you sleep an average of eight hours a day, then if you reach 100 years old you will have slept for over 33 years

Your skeleton isn't inside you. You are a brain which is inside your skull.

Our galaxy is going to crash into the Andromeda galaxy in about 5 billion years' time.

Melbourne gave some of its trees email addresses so residents could report problems. The residents prefer to send love letters to their trees.

Neil Armstrong's astronaut application arrived a week past the June 1st 1962 deadline. A friend, Dick Day, slipped the tardy form in with the others.

Route 66 can play a tune. If drivers stick to the 45 mph speed limit on a stretch of Route 66 in New Mexico, the road's rumble strips play a rendition of "America the Beautiful."

Space has a distinct smell, which is said to be like brake pads and walnuts.

The annual number of worldwide shark bites is 10 times less than the number of people bitten by other people in New York alone.

Barry Manilow did not write his hit song "I Write the Songs".

In 1983 Redondo Beach, California, adopted the Goodyear Blimp as 'the Official Bird of Redondo Beach'.

Marie Curie's notebooks are still radioactive after 100 years. Researchers opening the lead lined boxes must wear protective clothing and sign a waiver of liability.

If a human being's DNA were uncoiled, it would stretch 10 billion miles, which is the equivalent of going from Earth to Pluto and back.

The brain contains 86 billion nerve cells joined by 100 trillion connections.

Alaska is both the western- and easternmost state in the United States as it crosses the Longitude 180.

The fastest object ever made by man was a manhole cover which was used in a nuclear testing experiment. It is estimated to have left the ground at 37 miles per second

Black apples exist and are known as Black Diamond apples.

Scotland wanted a memorial to soldiers who died in the Napoleonic Wars. It was modelled on the Parthenon in 1826. It was never completed due to lack of funds and is now nicknamed "Scotland's Disgrace".

In Svalbard, a remote Norwegian island, it has been illegal to die since 1950.

Your kidneys filter about 1.2 litres per minute. All your blood is filtered more than 30 times every single day.

Everyone's face is crawling with eight-legged, spider-like creatures. Fortunately, they are microscopic and impossible to see

More people between 18 and 34 are living with their parents than on their own or with a partner for the first time in 130 years

Taking an aspirin at the first sign of a heart attack could be a lifesaver. The drug inhibits platelets from forming a clot that can block an artery and cause a full-on heart attack.

The first written instance of the name Jessica is found in Shakespeare's 1596 play The Merchant of Venice.

High heels were first designed for men. They were made for Persian soldiers in the 10th Century.

A group of pug dogs is called a grumble.

Before he became president, Abraham Lincoln was the wrestling champion of his county. He fought in nearly 300 matches and only lost one of them. He is in the Wrestling Hall of Fame.

Salvador Dalí avoided paying restaurant bills by using cheques. He would do a drawing on the back knowing that it would never be cashed.

A British man changed his name to Tim Pppppppppprice to make it harder for telemarketers to pronounce.

In 1965 'Slumber Party Barbie' came with pink scales set to 110lbs and a book called "How to Lose Weight." It came with one instruction "Don't eat."

The world's largest singular snowflake was 15 inches wide. This monster snowflake fell during a particularly bad snowstorm, over Montana in 1887

Astronauts cannot cry in space due to the lack of gravity. The tears just stick to the eyeball.

Saudi Arabia imports camels from Australia.

A loofa is a vegetable. It is a gourd.

Astronauts in orbit feel weightless because they are constantly falling, not because there is no gravity in orbit.

Honey never goes bad if you keep the lid on and don't add water.

Victoria Beckham paid £6,000 to British Airways so she could get off a plane first.

A chameleon's tongue is twice as long as its body.

A reindeer's eyes can change colour. They are golden in the summer, they shift to dark rich blue in the winter

There is an area of Canada has a weaker gravitational pull than the rest of Earth.

Since founding the Imagination Library in 1995, Dolly Parton has donated 100 million free books to children around the world.

In 1974, the Journal of Applied Behavior Analysis published a peer reviewed paper titled "The Unsuccessful Self-Treatment of a Case of Writer's Block." It contained a total of zero words. It received positive reviews

A teacher wrote of a young Roald Dahl on his school report card: "I have never met anybody who so persistently writes words meaning the exact opposite of what is intended".

The author of Winnie the Pooh, A.A. Milne, had a son called Christopher Robin.

Bono once bought a $1500 plane ticket just for his hat. He had forgotten it in Italy and wanted it back.

Marie Curie's body will continue to emit radiation for another 1500 years.

Wooden bathing suits were fashionable in the 1920s and helped buoyancy.

In 2006, magician David Copperfield tricked some would-be robbers into believing that he wasn't carrying anything although he had his wallet, phone, and passport.

Boring in Oregon, Dull in Scotland and Bland from Australia have been sister communities since 2012.

Ben & Jerry learned how to make ice cream by splitting the cost of a $5 correspondence course offered by Penn State.

Marie Curie remains the only person to earn Nobel prizes in two different sciences.

The bend in a flamingo's leg isn't a knee. It's an ankle.

Susan B. Anthony, the American social reformer, was fined $100 for voting in the 1872 election. She never paid the fine.

The collective noun for snails is a 'Walk'.

A Japanese brewery, Sankt Gallen, produces a beer called Un Kono Kuro, made with coffee beans that have passed through an elephant.

Researchers at John Hopkins University took the average of light from over 200,000 galaxies and found out the universe is, on average, beige. They named the colour "cosmic latte."

Air is 78 percent nitrogen and only 21% oxygen.

Around 3 - 4 billion years ago the moon had an atmosphere.

Ching Shih was the most successful pirate in history. She was an 19th century pirate and warlord

Toxoplasma gondii is a tiny parasite that can only breed sexually when in the guts of a cat. To achieve this when it infects rats, it changes their behaviour to make them less scared of cats.

The katzenklavier ("cat piano") was a musical instrument made using cats. Designed by 17th-century German scholar Athanasius Kircher, it consisted of a row of caged cats with different voice pitches.

There was an epidemic of contagious laughing that lasted almost a year in Tanganyika (now Tanzania) in 1962. Several thousand people were affected, across several villages. It forced a school to close.

There is enough gold at the core of the earth to cover the planet's surface to a depth of 4 metres, according to current theories. However, it's 1,800 miles below our feet and at many thousands of degrees.

Lemons float, but limes sink

Only 12 plants and five animal species make up 75% of the world's food.

The lining of your stomach turns red when you blush due to increased blood flow throughout the body.

In the 13th Century Pope Gregory IX declared that black cats were agents of the devil as they carried the spirit of Satan.

The poet Lord Byron had a pet bear at Cambridge University as the University had banned dogs.

Casu marzu is a Sardinian cheese that contains live maggots

Saudi Arabia is the largest country in the world without a permanent river.

In 2007, Iran arrested 14 squirrels for spying.

The Baobab Tree can store up to 32,000 gallons of water in its trunk.

Space is completely silent. As space is a vacuum, sound waves will have no medium to travel through.

The Titanic cost less to build even allowing for inflation, than the film Titanic cost to make.

Hawaii moves 7.5cm closer to Alaska every year

Trees have only been around for 360 million years, which is less than 10% of earth's entire history.

In 1912 Teddy Roosevelt was shot while he was campaigning but continued to finish his speech.

The world record for the longest jump by a human is greater than the world record for longest horse long jump.

Pigeon poop is the property of the British Crown. In the 18th century, pigeon poop was used to make gunpowder, so King George I confirmed the droppings to be the property of the Crown.

Plants have been shown to grow better when music is played

In 2007, an American named Corey Taylor tried to fake his own death to get out of his cell phone contract without paying a termination fee. It didn't work.

In 1567, Hans Steininger was said to have the longest beard in the world. He died after he tripped over his beard running away from a fire.

During World War II, the crew of the British submarine HMS Trident kept a fully grown reindeer called Pollyanna, a gift from the Russians, aboard their vessel for six weeks.

Ancient Greeks and Romans didn't have a number for zero.

Children of identical twins are genetically siblings, not cousins. Cousins whose parents are identical twins share 25 percent of their DNA, instead of the usual 12.5 percent. While full-siblings share 50 percent of their DNA, half-siblings share 25 percent.

The Angustopila Dominikae snail were discovered in 2014 and are just 0.03 inches (or 0.86 mm) tall. Ten of them could fit in the eye of a needle at the same time.

The Famous Easter Island heads have bodies which are hidden below ground.

The last man to walk on the moon was Gene Cernan. He promised his daughter he'd write her initials on the moon and left her initials, "TDC," in the moondust. They will probably still be there in thousands of years.

In the 1960s, the CIA tried to spy on the Russians by using cats. The project was called 'Acoustic Kitty', and involved implanting batteries, microphones and antennae inside cats.

All the clocks in the movie "Pulp Fiction" are stuck at 4:20.

When St. Louis held the 1904 Summer Olympic Games, events included greased pole climbing, rock throwing and mud fighting.

Leonardo Da Vinci's painting of the last supper included Jesus' feet, but they were cut off when a door was installed in the wall beneath the fresco in 1652.

The fax machine was patented by Scottish inventor Alexander Bain in 1843.

The word "unfriend" was first used in 1659.Thomas Fuller used the word in his book 'The Appeal of Injured Innocence'.

"Overmorrow" is the day after tomorrow.

The chance of you dying on the way to get lottery tickets is greater than your chance of winning the lottery.

Our eyes are always the same size from birth, but our nose and ears never stop growing.

The pharmaceutical company Bayer held the trademark for "heroin" and sold the drug as a cough and headache remedy

Robin chicks eat 14 feet of earthworms every day.

The chance of dying trying to climb Mt Everest is 3%

The Fulgates of Troublesome Creek of Kentucky had blue skin. This is thought to be the result of a combination of inbreeding and a rare genetic condition known as methemoglobinemia.

The top of the Eiffel Tower leans away from the sun, as the metal facing the sun heats up and expands. It can move up to 7 inches.

A U.S. park ranger named Roy C. Sullivan held the record for being struck by lightning the most times, having been struck seven times between 1942 and 1977. He survived all the strikes.

Google hires a flock of 200 goats to chew away the grass on their lawns rather than using lawn mowers.

There is a black rose. Black roses exist naturally only in Halfeti, Turkey.

The Centennial Light is the world's longest glowing light bulb. It was installed in 1901 and has been burning for over 120 years. It is installed in Livermore, California

The Sun will engulf Earth in 5 billion years as it turns into a red giant.

About 1.4 billion years ago, a day on Earth was just 18 hours 41 minutes long as the moon was closer to the earth.

Scotland has 421 words for snow

"Running amok" is a medically recognized mental condition.

Blue whales eat half a million calories in one mouthful in the form of small shrimplike krill.

Stephen Spielberg didn't impress the film school at the University of Southern California. In fact, the university reportedly rejected Spielberg three times.

Apple fired Steve Jobs from his own company, though they took him back on.

Your stomach acid is strong enough to dissolve metal.

When you are born you have just 1 pint of blood, but by the time you're an adult you have about 10 pints.

The pressure in the deepest part of the ocean is 1100 times greater than on the surface

The world's largest waterfall is underwater between Iceland and Greenland and called the Denmark Strait. The water falls 11,500 feet.

Camels have three eyelids and two rows of eyelashes to keep sand out.

Clownfish are all born male but can morph into females as necessary. The process can be reversed.

T. S. Eliot wore green makeup

Theodore Roosevelt had a pet hyena called Bill. It was a gift from the Emperor of Ethiopia.

Beethoven never knew how to multiply or divide. He went to a Latin school where he was taught some math but never learned multiplication or division, only addition

After dropping out of his school in Munich at 15, Einstein flunked the entrance exam for a polytechnic school in Zurich.

The fastest growing plant is bamboo. It can shoot up 35 inches each day

The Megaphragma mymaripenne wasp is the smallest wasp in the world and measures a fifth of a millimetre and is smaller than many one-cell amoebas.

FDA regulations allow 10 insects and 35 fruit fly eggs per 8 ounces of raisins.

You can tell the difference between hot and cold water by listening to it.

Crocodiles and alligators can climb trees.

If you google 241503903 you will see lots of images of people putting their heads in the freezer.

New York is about 100km further south than Rome.

Wombats poop cubes.

A 'buttload' is an actual measurement and is 126 gallons.

Babies cry in the womb.

You can't breathe and swallow at the same time.

The odds of being born with 11 fingers or toes are 1 in 500.

Being a twin is becoming more common. The rate has gone up from 2% to about 3.3% in the last 40 years.

Dragons Breath Chili is the hottest chili and eating one could be fatal by burning your airways and causing anaphylactic shock.

The average adult is 5 feet 1.8 inches in Indonesia.

The odds of being injured by a toilet is 1 in 10,000.

Four babies are born every second

There are more than 24 time zones.

There is a website that tracks the world population in real time.

The odds of being struck by lightning are 1 in 11,195

The highest speed ever achieved on a bicycle is 166.94 mph, by Fred Rompelberg of the Netherlands

The oceans contain enough salt to cover all the continents to a depth of nearly 500 feet.

Truman Show Syndrome is a psychological disorder where people believe they are stars in a reality TV show.

We are all made of stardust. Almost every element on Earth was created in the core of a star therefore our bodies are made from stardust.

Dead skin cells are a main ingredient in household dust

For those who want an environmentally sound ending there's a company that turns dead bodies into an ocean reef.

Alfred Hitchcock was frightened of eggs.

Mayor Stubbs was the mayor of the Alaskan town of Talkeetna for 20 years. Mayor Stubs was a cat.

In ancient Greece and Rome, doctors used spider webs to make bandages for their patients.

Sunglasses were originally made from quartz for Chinese judges to hide their facial expressions in court.

A cornflake in the shape of Illinois was sold on eBay for $1,350.

The Apollo 11 crew were uninsurable in the case of them being killed on the mission to the moon. To provide for their families they signed cards to be sold by their families in the event of an accident. Today these cards sell for between $10 – 40,000.

All the swans in England are owned by the king and are counted in a process called swan upping.

The Kamchatka meteor exploded over the Bering Sea on December 18th, 2018. It exploded with a force of 10 Hiroshima bombs. Turns out, it went largely undetected because it took place over the Bering Sea

Louisiana is home to a rare pink dolphin named Pinky. The pink coloration is likely due to a genetic condition.

A "moonbow" is a rainbow that happens at night.

Octopuses have a top speed of up to 25 miles per hour.

Australia has pink and purple lakes.

The "placebo effect" is the beneficial effect that a patient gets from the administration of a substance which will have no medical benefit. The reasons for the beneficial effect are poorly understood.

Moon dust is said to smell like gunpowder

You always see the same side of the Moon. This is because the moon rotates on its axis in the same time it takes to orbit the Earth.

Dogs can sniff at the same time as breathing.

The cornea is the only part of the body with no blood supply. It gets oxygen directly from the air.

According to scientist Dr Roger Clark the human eye has about 576 megapixels or resolution

You carry, on average, about four pounds of bacteria around in your body, which is enough to fill a large soup can.

All Panama hats are made in Ecuador.

Roselle, a guide dog, lead her blind owner down 78 flights of stairs of the North Tower of the World Trade Centre on 9/11.

When you burn fat, it metabolizes to become carbon dioxide, water, and energy. This means you exhale the fat that you lose.

If you ate nothing but rabbit meat, you would die from protein poisoning.

A horse is capable of a peak production of 14.9 horsepower.

During WWII, the British Navy destroyed the French fleet on July 3rd 1940 after France fell to Germany in WW II.

QWERTY keyboards were originally designed to slow down typing so that the strikers didn't get locked up.

In 1912 a French orphanage held a raffle, with the consent of the authorities, with babies as the prize.

Farm-raised salmon is dyed pink otherwise it would be grey.

Nikola Tesla, who had fallen on hard times, once paid for a hotel bill with a 'death ray of unimaginable power'. He told the employees not to open the box due to the danger.

In 1915, the lock millionaire Cecil Chubb bought his wife Stonehenge for £6,600 at auction. She didn't like it, so in 1918 he gave it to the nation.

Jimmy Carter once sent a jacket to the cleaners with the nuclear detonation codes still in the pocket.

John Cleese's father's surname was originally Cheese.

In 1811, nearly a quarter of all the women in Britain were named Mary.

Amazon used to be called Relentless.

The peacock mantis shrimp has the world's fastest punch at speeds of 23m/sec.

A Narwhal tusk is a canine tooth.

Several species of terrestrial snails have hairy shells.

Zebra stripes act as a natural bug repellant.

Frogs can freeze without dying.

Baseball legend Babe Ruth wore a cabbage leaf that he had put in an ice box under his cap to keep his head cool.

In 1999, Darlington FC acquired 50,000 worms to improve drainage at their flooded pitch. Unfortunately, they all drowned.

Percussive maintenance is the term for hitting a piece of equipment till it works.

Monarch butterflies see you through their 12,000 eyes.

Applying lemon juice onto freckles fades them and makes them less noticeable.

Google used to be called BackRub back in 1996.

Sign language has tongue twisters. They are called finger fumblers.

A survey found that there are 13.61 million households in the USA with a net worth of more than $1 million.

A snail can have 20,000 teeth.

Children's book author, Roald Dahl was a British spy during World War II

The most widely printed book in the world is the IKEA catalogue. Over 200 million copies of its catalogue are printed annually.

When you crack your knuckles, the noise is created by nitrogen gas bubbles compressing and bursting.

McDonald's once had bubble-gum flavoured broccoli to encourage children to eat more healthily.

In the 90s North Korean teachers were required to play the accordion. This musical instrument is also known as the "people's instrument" and was very convenient for taking to marches.

Bottled water has an expiration date. The expiration date is for the bottle itself which can be between 6 months and 2 years, and not the water.

Charles Darwin's pet turtle outlived him and lived to be 176 years old and died in 2006.

The Firefox logo isn't a fox. The logo is a red panda.

When the first VCR (Video Camera Recorder) was made in 1956, it was the size of a piano.

When you click to agree to the Terms & Conditions for iTunes, one of the conditions you are agreeing to is not to use it to make nuclear weapons.

People in Victorian Britain who couldn't afford chimney sweeps dropped live geese down their chimneys instead.

Thomas Adams made the first commercial chewing gum in 1871. This was after he had failed to make cheap car tires from the same ingredients.

In his first year at Harrow, Winston Churchill was bottom of the whole school.

The Romans used urine as a tooth-cleaning agent.

Margaret Thatcher was a member of the research team that invented whippy ice cream

In 1252, King Henry III received a polar bear as a gift from Norway. He kept it in the Tower of London and allowed it to swim in the Thames to catch fish.

Queen Elizabeth II is related to Vlad The Impaler, a medieval Romanian king who was known for his brutality and love of impaling people. He became the inspiration for Bram Stoker's Dracula.

Ludwig Van Beethoven was profoundly deaf. His last words were "I shall hear in Heaven".

People used to answer the phone with "ahoy".

Dragonflies are not capable of walking. Their legs are too weak for them to walk.

Baby octopuses are the size of a flea.

A scorpion can hold its breath for a week.

Chocolate can kill dogs.

A "feral child" is a human who has been raised by animals. There have been more than 100 documented cases of this so far and they have been raised from animals ranging from monkeys to goats.

If you rub an onion on your foot, you'll be able to taste it within 30-60 minutes because it travels through the blood stream.

A prison in the small Brazilian state of minas Gerais allows inmates to pedal on exercise bikes to power lights in a nearby town in exchange for reduced sentences. For every 8 hour shift they get one day off.

A study in the New England Journal of Medicine shows right handed people live, on average, nine years longer than left-handed people

A snail can go into prolonged dormancy for 3 – 4 years during which period it does not need food

The academic journal Science says that data centres use 1% of the world's generated energy.

Your monthly data requests while using the internet generate about the same amount of greenhouse gas emissions as driving a car one mile.

The Formula 1 driver Lewis Hamilton's dog Roscoe earns $700 a day as a dog model.

2020 Tokyo Olympic medals are made from recycled electronic items including phones. Citizens in Japan donated 78,985 tons of old electronic devices from which 66.8 pounds of gold, 9,039 pounds of silver, and 5,952 pounds of bronze were extracted

Each year, a single cow will belch about 220 pounds of methane, which is shorter lived than carbon dioxide but 28 times more potent in warming the atmosphere.

Planarian flatworms can regrow an entire body from a single remaining cell.

The world's largest wind turbine is in the Netherlands and stand 260m tall. It takes just one spin to power the average home for 2 days.

Viruses exist in the atmosphere and fall to Earth every day. Researchers at the British Columbia University found around 800 million viruses fall per square metre from the sky each day.

Turkeys are capable of virgin birth. A female can produce offspring without sex, but they will all be males.

There are 788 billionaires in the USA

Male horses have an average of 40 permanent teeth, while females have an average of 36.

Octopuses can taste with their arms.

Adult cats only meow at humans and not to each other.

Humans have about 9,000 taste buds, while dogs have only around 1,700.

Otters have the world's thickest fur. They're thought to have up to one million hairs per square inch.

Whales used to have four legs and live on land.

Elephants fear ants.

Horyuji, a Buddhist temple in Japan, is currently the world's oldest wooden building at 1400 years old.

The world's longest bridge is in China and is 168.4km long.

You can get a 3D printed house.

Hospitals in Japan omit 4th and 9th floors because the four sounds like 'death' and nine sounds like 'pain' in Japanese.

The Dingo Fence in Australia is 5,614km long.

The larvae of wax moths eat plastic.

Table forks were banned by the church as they believed it was a diabolic tool, and people already had fingers to eat with.

Ants can survive in a microwave. They are small enough to dodge the rays.

A candle's flame is hot, round and blue in zero gravity.

Putting sugar on a cut will make it heal faster. Sugar draws water from the wound into the dressing accelerating the healing process.

The record for laying bricks is 915 per hour and was set in 1987 by American bricklayer Bob Boil. That is one every 4 seconds.

Steel wool gets heavier when you burn it.

Rolls Royce makes its own honey. It has 250,000 bees in its UK workforce.

Octopuses have three hearts.

Your nose is always in your field of vision, but your brain filters it out through a process called Unconscious Selective Attention.

In a 2019 study published in Scientific Reports, researchers discovered that while cats can distinguish their own name, they feel under no obligation to respond.

There are 7 different types of twins. Apart from the well-known identical and fraternal types of twins, there are 5 more. These include half-identical, mirror image, mixed, chromosome, superfecundation, and superfetation.

The only innate fears we have at birth, regardless of culture, are the fear of falling and loud noises.

June and Jennifer Gibbons were identical twins and grew up in Wales. They were known as "The Silent Twins" as they only communicated with each other.

There's a particle accelerator in the Louvre's basement. It is used to determine which elements are in a particular artwork.

There were 17,500 square miles of adhesive tape manufactured in 2018, enough to completely cover Denmark

The first recorded baseball game took place in Walton-on-Thames in England in 1749. The Prince of Wales and the Earl of Middlesex played in it.

Placebo's work best for women if the pill is blue and best for men if it is orange.

Oscar statuettes are owned by the Academy or must be sold back to them for $1.

Recycling an aluminium can into a new one takes only 5% of the energy required to produce one from bauxite.

At least 80% of our sense of taste comes from our sense of smell.

In 1913 you could legally mail a baby in the US, and it seemed to have happened more than once.

Jupiter has a "lost" moon. S/2003 J 10 has been 'lost' due to its uncertain orbit. It was discovered in 2003 and has not been seen since.

Famous French painter Claude Monet lived with financial troubles. In 1890 he won 100,000 francs, which is about $340,000 today. This allowed him to do as he wished.

The 'Spanish Flu' pandemic of 1918 claimed between 17 and 50 million lives, which is more than died in World War 1

Russia defrosted some worms collected from the permafrost in the Arctic. After they thawed out, two of the worms started moving and eating. One is 32,000 years old, and the other is 41,700 years old.

Reindeer in the Arctic can see ultraviolet light.

Heinrich Hertz proved the existence of radio waves, but thought they were completely pointless.

The only window that opens on the presidential car is the driver's window, to pay tolls. It also has no keyholes.

Joseph Stalin had webbed feet. He had a condition called syndactyly.

The gravity in a neutron star is so strong, it can bend light so that you see all sides of the star at once.

The highest number of aircraft recorded flying in any 24 hour period is over 220,000 in 2019

44% of all Bitcoin transactions are estimated to be illegal transactions.

Row 13 does not exist on Air France, Iberia, Ryanair, AirTran, Continental Airlines and Lufthansa. Presumably it would be difficult tickets to sell in row 13.

Adult Mayflies have no mouth.

In 2011 scientists at the Mayo clinic used a fluorescent protein from a specific jellyfish when testing for a gene in cats. The tests were a success, but the cats did end up glowing in the dark.

Mock naval battles were sometimes held in Rome's Colosseum. The Romans would sometimes flood the Colosseum with water from a nearby aqueduct. The first was given by Julius Caesar to celebrate his triumphs.

Until 1857, it was legal for British husbands to sell their wives. Between 1780 and 1850 around 300 wives were sold.

Hedy Lamarr as well as being leading actress was a gifted mathematician and physicist. She helped to develop a technology for a radio guidance system for torpedoes.

The principles of the technology were incorporated into Bluetooth.

Oneironaut literally means 'dream traveller'. It is the ability to travel in your dreams on a conscious basis.

Gold bar vending machines exist

During the height of Tulipmania in 1635, a sale of 40 bulbs sold for 100,000 Dutch guilders. A skilled labourer might earn 150–350 guilders a year.

One of Queen Victoria's wedding presents was a 3 metre wide cheese that weighed half a ton.

Dogs, cats, ferrets, hedgehogs and okapi can all see ultraviolet light.

Saint Julian, the Hospitaller's saint. is also the patron saint of clowns, fiddle players and murderers.

Subway used to be called Pete's Super Submarines and opened in 1965.

Fewer than 60 people have been born on an aeroplane. The first was in 1927 where the couple purposefully circled at 2000 feet until they gave birth. They called their baby "Airleen".

There are at least 373 women and girls named Abcde in the United States according to Social Security records.

Producing a single Kg of beef needs 15,000 litres of water. Producing 1kg of rice needs only 2,000 litres.

A gallon of scorpion venom would cost you $39 million.

Uncombable hair syndrome is a thing caused by a mutation usually developed in childhood.

The Wife Carrying World Championships have been held annually since 1992 in Finland. If you win the prize offered is your wife's weight in beer.

Carolyn Davidson designed the iconic Nike swoosh trademark in 1971. She was paid $35 after working on it for 17.5 hours.

Nicolas Mahut and John Isner played the longest tennis match in history. It finished 70-68 in the 5th set after 11 hours and five minutes.

Drinking absolutely pure water will kill you.

The average time for a baby to be born spontaneously in England is 4am. The majority arrive between 1am and 7am.

Decorations and Christmas trees are banned in public places in Brunei. Anyone breaking this law is liable to a five-year jail sentence.

The Mpemba Effect is when water which is hot freezes quicker than cold water.

An octopus has nine brains. It has one central brain, and eight smaller brains located in each of its arms.

1 percent of the static you see on your TV is attributed to the Big Bang.

Scientists have recorded a video of jumping spiders moving their legs while asleep suggesting that they're in a state resembling REM sleep and likely dreaming.

Kangaroos can't walk backwards.

Turning the thermostat down just 1°C saves 8% in heating costs on average.

Bir Tawil is an area of 795.4 sq. miles between Egypt and Sudan that is claimed by neither country.

The first book ever to be ordered by an online customer of Amazon was "Douglas Hofstadter's Fluid Concepts and Creative Analogies." It was ordered on April 3rd 1995.

Brisbane in Australia hosts the cockroach racing world championship.

The Platypus and the Echidna are the only two mammals in the world that lay eggs to give birth.

It is physically impossible for pigs to look up into the sky.

The bulletproof kevlar vest was invented by a pizza delivery guy Richard Davis, from Detroit USA, after he was shot twice on the job. During testing he shot himself 190 times in the chest.

Every planet of the whole solar system could physically fit between the earth and the moon if we ignore gravity.

Two 12-inch pizzas are smaller in size than one 18-inch pizza.

The Mona Lisa was in Napoleon Bonaparte's bedroom for four years.

If you make ice cubes with tap water, they will be white; if you use boiled water, they will be transparent. Boiling water removes the gases in the solution prior to freezing.

An Ipsos poll found that globally one in every five adults believe that aliens are hiding on Earth disguised as humans.

According to NASA 84% of lightening fatalities are men.

It's not uncommon for deaf people to use sign language in their sleep

Those born blind experience dreams involving things such as emotion, sound and smell rather than sight

Within 5 minutes of waking up, 50% of your dream is forgotten and within 10 minutes 90% is gone.

The world's largest wheat fields are in Canada. The largest single fenced field was in the province of Alberta and sown with wheat in 1951 and measured 35,000 acres.

4 of the 5 most dangerous cities in the world ranked by murder rate are in Mexico. Tijuana in Mexico is the worst with 138 murders per 100,000 people.

Leonardo da Vinci could write with one hand and draw with the other at the same time.

A flea can jump 200 times its body length, the equivalent of a human jumping the length of four football fields.

Coca-Cola would be green if colouring wasn't added to it.

According to the UN going to work is statistically more dangerous than war, drug and alcohol abuse combined.

More than 2 million people die from work related accidents or disease every year.

President Harry S. Truman (1945-1953) The "S" in Harry S. Truman was just an initial. It didn't stand for any name. The same as Ulysses S. Grant didn't stand for anything either.

A typical microwave uses more electricity to keep its digital clock on standby than it does heating food. When the microwave is heating it uses 100 times as much power as running the clock, but it is often on standby for 99% of the time.

In the average home, 75% of the electricity used to power electronics is consumed while the products are turned off (on standby).

There is a mountain called Mt Disappointment in Australia. It is so named because early European explorers were disappointed with the view.

Melbourne was named Batmania for two years. It was named after the local politician John Batman.

2% of people dream entirely in black and white.

There are no seagulls in Hawaii.

To make one pound of honey, honeybees must gather nectar from nearly 2 million flowers. This requires the bees to travel 55 km

Termite queens live longer than any other insect. Some scientists estimate that they can live 50 years.

The Shin Kicking World Championship in 2022 has been saved after a £5,000 grant from Gloucestershire County Council

Isaac Newton was a member of the British parliament for one year. Perhaps the greatest mind in history made only one contribution to parliament, and that was to tell someone to please close the window.

According to Google, the energy it takes to conduct 100 searches on its site is equivalent to a 60-watt light bulb burning for 28 minutes

Bee Hummingbirds are the smallest birds in the world. They are so minuscule that they are sometimes mistaken for insects which explains their name, according to the National Audubon Society. The birds are just 6cm long and weigh about 2 grams.

Explorer James Cook discovered Sandy Island in 1774 in the Pacific Ocean, and it began appearing on nautical maps in 1908. It wasn't until 2012, when a team of Australian scientists set out to survey the island, that they discovered that it didn't exist.

According to the Centers for Disease Control, cows kill around 22 people per year.

On average Germany uncovers 2,000 tons of unexploded bombs every year.

Sharks existed before trees. Sharks have existed for around 400 million years, while trees became their own official species only 350 million years ago

A ripped dollar bill still has its face value, if the remaining piece is larger than half.

The Sentinel Andaman Island is a secluded island in the Andaman Sea ear India. The Sentinelese people who live on the North of the island reject any contact with the outside world. They are the last people who remain untouched by the modern civilization and are prone to kill intruders.

The Golden Poison Dart Frog is likely the most poisonous animal and has enough toxin to kill 20 people.

You cannot snore and dream at the same time

Chewing gum while you cut an onion will help keep you from crying by forcing you to breathe through the mouth.

The word "gorilla" is derived from a Greek word meaning, "A tribe of hairy women."

A waterfall in Hawaii sometimes goes up instead of down. It is not an optical illusion but because of the extreme wind.

A ten-gallon hat will only hold ¾ of a gallon.

The male ostrich can roar just like a lion.

Cat's urine glows under a black light

Beetles taste like apples, wasps like pine nuts, and worms like fried bacon apparently.

The Greek national anthem has 158 verses

In France, it is legal to marry a dead person if you apply to the President.

The Barreleye fish has a transparent dome like head. This is so it can see the silhouettes of prey above it.

The cruise liner, Queen Elizabeth II, moves only six inches for each gallon of diesel that it burns.

The very first bomb dropped by the Allies on Berlin during World War II Killed the only elephant in the Berlin Zoo.

Hot water is heavier than cold, because as Einstein told us E=mc2. So, if E, the energy in the water, goes up because it's hotter then mass, m, must also go up to keep the equation balanced

The kangaroo mouse never needs to drink water as it gets all the moisture it needs from its food.

Greenland sharks don't reach sexual maturity until they're 150 according to a study in Journal Science.

According to the BBC, a Swedish couple once tried to name their child Brfxxccxxmnpcccclllmmnprxvclmnckssqlbb11116, which is apparently pronounced "Albin." This was to protest Sweden's strict name-related laws, which is why their selection was rejected.

Anne Frank and Martin Luther King, Jr. were born in 1929.

The U.S. government has an official plan for a zombie apocalypse. It is named Conplan 8888 and the first line is 'This plan was not actually designed as a joke'.

A Bengal tiger called the Champawat Man-eater killed an estimated 436 people at the turn of the 20th century.

Sesame seeds were once worth more than gold in the Middle Ages.

Samuel J. Seymour was just five years old when he attended a play at Ford's Theater on that fateful evening of April 14, 1865 when President Lincoln was assassinated. On February 9, 1956, two months before his death, Seymour recounted the story on the CBS TV show 'I've Got a Secret'.

Graham's number is a number so large that a digital representation of it cannot be contained in the observable universe.

At the end of World War 2 the USA had 16,000,000 service personnel. There were 11,200,000 in the army, 4,200,000 in the navy and 660,000 in the marine corps

Despite its hump, camels have straight spines.

There's a town called "Big Ugly" in West Virginia

According to NASA the fastest a raindrop will fall is 10 metres a second.

A pigeon's feathers weigh more than their bones. Its bones are hollow and therefore very light.

Japan has a phone to call the dead. It is in a booth on a hill overlooking the Pacific Ocean and is called the 'phone of the wind'.

The phrase "umop apisdn" is "upside down" spelled upside down.

The first sliced bread was sold on July 7th 1928 in Chillicothe Missouri.

All mammals have seven vertebra in their necks apart from sloths and manatees.

"Shemomechama" is a useful Georgian word which means "I accidentally ate the whole thing."

The light from stars doesn't really twinkle. It is the Earth's atmosphere distorting the light making them appear to twinkle.

There is a museum in California dedicated to failure. It has exhibits such as fingerless gloves, Harley-Davidson perfume and plain Oreos (without the cream).

The youngest Olympian to ever become a medallist is Greek gymnast Dimitrios Loundras, who finished third at the 1896 Olympic Games when he was 10 years old.

Le Palais Idéal is an 85-foot-long, 33-foot-high whimsical castle 30 miles south of Lyon. It is made from rocks that a 19th-century French postman picked up during his mail route over the course of 34 years.

All five of George Foreman's sons have the same name, George Foreman. "I named all my sons George Edward Foreman so they would always have something in common" he said.

There are more McDonalds restaurants in the USA than hospitals.

A war was ostensibly started by a football game. In 1969, the soccer teams of Honduras and El Salvador were competing for a spot in the 1970 World Cup. El Salvador won a playoff after extra time and violence escalated from there, though there were underlying tensions.

Pistol shrimp can make a sound louder than a gun and kill prey using bubbles. The sound of the bubble has been measured at 210 decibels.

In the early 1900s, Lobster was considered the "cockroach of the ocean" and was often eaten by the homeless, slaves, and prisoners.

Every 'c' in Pacific Ocean is pronounced differently.

There are now giant pigs being bred in China as heavy as polar bears. They weigh 500kg.

Golfers can get hole-in-one insurance and it costs between $200 - $1,000. It is to pay the subsequent bar bill.

A 135-square-foot parking spot in front of Hong Kong's fifth tallest building, The Center, was purchased for $969,000.

Household-cleaner Cillit Bang was used to clean plutonium stains away in the Dounreay nuclear power plant in Scotland as it was being dismantled.

The word 'deadline' comes from the American Civil War. Prisoners would have lines drawn around them in the dirt, and if they crossed this line then they would be shot by their guards.

Take Your Houseplants for a Walk Day is celebrated on July 27th every year. On this day, people walk their houseplants around.

Alfredo Moser invented a lamp in 2002. He used a plastic bottle filled with water and fitted it through his roof. It works by refraction of sunlight and produces similar brightness to a 40- to 60-watt incandescent bulb during the hours of daylight. It uses no electricity or power other than natural light

Goosebumps are caused by muscles.

There is a blind man in America, Daniel Kish, who uses echolocation to navigate in the same way as a bat. He does this by producing a clicking sound with his tongue and then listening as the sound waves bounce back.

Approximately 1,000,000 dogs in the U.S. are named as the primary beneficiaries of their owners' wills.

To drink a cat laps liquid from the underside of its tongue rather than the top.

In a survival situation if you were to drink seawater you would rapidly dehydrate and soon lead to your death. However, if you eat frozen seawater it is much less harmful. This is because frozen seawater contains a tenth the amount of salt as its liquid form

In Canada, 2012, doctors were able to communicate with a man in a vegetative state. Coma patient Scott Routley was able to tell doctors by using his thoughts that he was not in any pain.

The South African railway once employed a baboon in Uitenhage in the Cape as a signalman. His name was Jack, and he never once made a mistake.

46 BC was 445 days long and is the longest year in human history. Nicknamed the year of confusion, this year had three extra leap months inserted by Julius Caesar. This was to make his new Julian Calendar match up with the seasonal year.

Hollywood moved from New York to Los Angeles to escape Edison's patents. Thomas Edison owned the Motion Pictures Patents Company which had most of the technology patents needed to make movies.

Charles Darwin invented the wheeled office chair. He used it to examine different specimens in his office.

The Voynich Manuscript is a manuscript which has been dated to the early 15th century. It consists of around 240 pages, is written in an unknown language, and has never been deciphered.

The Vikings discovered America 500 years before Christopher Columbus. The Viking chief Leif Eriksson of Greenland landed on the Island of Newfoundland in the year 1,000 AD.

Mosquitoes kill nearly 1 million people every year.

Drug lord Pablo Escobar spent $2500 a month on rubber bands to hold all his cash.

Clams have feet. Inside their shell they have a retractable foot which they use to bury themselves.

The Atlantic Ocean is saltier than the Pacific Ocean. This is due to the higher evaporation in the Atlantic which leaves a greater salt concentration.

A new-born baby is 78 percent water. Adults are 55-60 percent water.

There wasn't just one Ice Age. There may have been at least 5 different Ice Ages in the past. It is believed that between 2.4 billion and 580 million years ago the earth was covered in ice to the equator. This period is known as 'Snowball Earth'.

A sunset is usually more spectacular than a sunrise because of the dust and particles that are thrown up by the sun heating the ground creating thermals. The dust then refracts the light and creates the sunsets we love.

Helicopters do not take off or land by changing the speed of the rotor blades. The rotor blades are always moving at the exact same speed. It is the angle of the blades that changes.

Police in the central Indian state of Madhya Pradesh are paid an extra 66 cents a month (30 rupees) for having a moustache. It is believed to give them an air of authority.

In 1941, during World War II, a Great Dane named Juliana was awarded the Blue Cross Medal. She extinguished an incendiary bomb by peeing on it. Juliana was celebrated as a hero.

A group of ravens is called an unkindness.

President Andrew Jackson had a pet parrot, and he taught his parrot, Polly, to curse like a sailor. The parrot had to be removed from Jackson's funeral due to its language.

Between November 1944 and April 1945 Japan launched 9,300 balloons with high explosives attached to fly over the Pacific Ocean and land in the USA. In 1945, a balloon bomb in Oregon caused the death of a woman and five children, who died when it exploded while they were having a picnic. These were the only World War II casualties on US soil.

Our brains (unintentionally) believe what we want to believe. Humans are victim to something called confirmation bias, which is the tendency to interpret facts in a way that confirms what we already believe.

The Oxford English Dictionary has estimated that Shakespeare invented more than 1,700 words?

Extreme ironing is apparently a sport. Participants are called 'ironists'.

The first item sold on eBay was a broken laser pointer that sold for $14.83

Grapes will catch fire in the microwave.

In a 100 years period, on average, a water molecule will spend 98 years in the oceans, 20 months as ice, about 2 weeks in lakes and rivers and less than a week in the atmosphere.

The sound made by the Krakatoa volcanic eruption in 1883 was so loud it ruptured eardrums of people 40 miles away. The sound was 310 decibels.

During the Soviet-era rule of the late 20th century, simply mentioning the great Mongolian Genghis Khan's name was a crime against the USSR. The Soviets removed his story from school textbooks and outlawed pilgrimages to his birthplace of Khentii.

The Colosseum was originally clad entirely in marble. When you visit the Colosseum these days, you'll notice how the stone exterior appears to be covered in pockmarks all across its surface. This is where the Goths removed the marble when they ransacked Rome.

The Leaning Tower of Pisa was never straight. It started sinking as they built it and they tried to adjust the design to compensate. It is impossible to 'straighten' the Leaning Towe of Pisa'.

The earliest ever lottery was during the Chinese Han Dynasty between 205 – 187 BC.

Roman Emperor Gaius, also known as Caligula, made one of his favorite horses a senator. The emperor loved his horse, named Incitatus.

If we have a plan B, our plan A is less likely to work. In a series of experiments from the University of Pennsylvania, researchers found that when volunteers thought about a backup plan before starting a task, they did worse than those who hadn't thought about a plan B.

Our brains have something called a "negativity bias" that makes us remember bad news more than good

A team from North Carolina State University studied the belly buttons of 60 different people and they found a "rain forest" of microscopic life. In total, they identified 2,368 bacterial species, 1,458 of which may be new.

Our bodies emit light in very small quantities. The intensity of the light emitted by the body is 1,000 times lower than the sensitivity of our naked eyes.

Pieces of the same metal become permanently stuck together if they touch in space. This is thanks to something called "cold welding." This was discovered during 1965's Gemini IV mission when astronauts were temporarily unable to close a hatch after a spacewalk because the door's metals had fused when exposed to space.

According to the Chicago Historical Society, the term "Windy City" was first coined by 19th century journalists to describe the people who find themselves in the city's elite who were "full of hot air."

One would assume that dying of thirst and dehydration would be the leading cause of death in the desert, but surprisingly, it's drowning, according to the United States Geological Survey.

According to historians, the first emperor to die from elixir poisoning was Qin Shi Huang around 210 B.C. These elixirs contained mercury, lead, and arsenic, and resulted in their deaths from poisoning.

Adolf Hitler plotted to kill Winston Churchill with exploding chocolate. The explosives were coated with a thin layer of chocolate. The plot was foiled though.

New York was briefly named "New Orange" when the Dutch captured New York from the English in 1673. They renamed it New Orange in honour of William III of Orange. The following year, the English regained control and ditched the "Orange".

The blob of toothpaste that sits on your toothbrush has a name. It's called a "nurdle," and there was a lawsuit over which toothpaste company had the right to use the word.

King Tutankhamun had a dagger, discovered in his tomb in 1925, made of meteoric metal. The dagger's composition of iron, nickel, and cobalt "strongly suggests an extra-terrestrial origin."

Colombian drug-lord Pablo Escobar kept four Hippos in his estate before his death in 1993. Deemed too much hassle to move by authorities, his Hippos were left there and have since bred and escaped becoming an invasive species of Colombia.

Vladimir Pravik was one of the first firefighters to reach the Chernobyl Nuclear Power Plant on April 26th, 1986. The radiation was so strong that it changed his eye color from brown to blue. He died sixteen days later.

The Luftwaffe had a master interrogator whose tactic was being as nice as possible. Hanns Scharff's best tactics for squeezing information out of prisoners included: nature walks without guards present, baking them homemade food, cracking jokes, drinking beers, and afternoon tea.

Shrapnel is named after British Army Officer Henry Shrapnel who was the first person to invent a new artillery shell that could transport a large number of bullets to its target before releasing them.

If you grind a marine sponge through a sieve into salt water, it'll reorganize itself back into a sponge. It's the only animal that we know of that can do that

Veronica Seider has extraordinary eyesight. Visual acuity in the normal human eyes is 20/20, whereas Veronica's was about 20/2. She could easily and quickly recognise individuals from one mile away.

Snails can regenerate their eyes.

The German word "Kummerspeck" literally translates to "grief bacon". It refers to weight gain due to emotional eating

If you type the word "askew" into the Google search box, the entire page will tilt slightly.

After the 9/11 attack on the World Trade Center, the East African Masai Tribe, gave 14 Cows to help the United States recover. The animals, which are considered sacred by the Masai, were presented to the US Embassy in Kenya.

Genetic research has shown that Madagascar was founded about 1200 years ago by a small group of about 30 women of mostly south east Asian heritage.

Monaco's orchestra is bigger than its army.

Tennis was originally played in France with bare hands. It was called 'the game of the palm'.

Baby mice are sometimes called pinkies

The technical term for a fear of long words is 'hippopotomonstrosesquippedaliophobia'.

Comets in ancient Greece were called "hairy stars" in reference to the tail which looks like hair.

African lions catch about 20% of the prey they chase. Dragonflies catch 95%. Dragonflies are the world's deadliest hunters.

Space is only about 62 miles away from the surface of the earth. This is called the Kármán line.

Light can travel 1,000 metres into the ocean under the right conditions. However, there is rarely much light beyond 200 metres. This led scientists to believe that no life existed past this point.

Jellyfish have existed on earth for between 500 and 700 million years.

Research suggests that blue, green, and hazel eyes all exist thanks to a genetic mutation. Brown was the only eye colour present in humans until about 10,000 years ago.

Human brains have shrunk 17.4% for over the last 20,000 years

In the US women couldn't apply for credit at a bank until the Equal Opportunities Credit Act of 1974.

None of The Beatles could read music. However, George Harrison could play 26 instruments.

Danish physicist Lene Hau was able to slow down the speed of light to about 17 metres per second.

French women were banned from dressing like a man and wearing trousers in 1800. This law was repealed in 2013.

In the USA the Internal Revenue Service seized $3.5 billion worth of cryptocurrencies during the fiscal year 2021. This was about 93% of all assets seized.

The First McDonald's Drive-Thru was intended for soldiers who were unable to leave their vehicles while in uniform.

Spitfire Planes were Crowdfunded During World War II. The public funding raised £13m which is the equivalent of over £600m today.

Kriegspiel chess is a variant of chess developed by Henry Michael Temple. Players can see their own pieces but not the opponents. It is meant to replicate a real war situation.

Penicillin was discovered by accident by Alexander Fleming in 1928.

Eyeglasses were invented in the 13th century in Italy.

The human body is comprised of the same quantity of energy as 10 hydrogen bombs

When you gain or lose weight, your fat cells don't disappear — they just change their size.

The Letter J was invented for the Italian language by a man called "Gian Giorgio Trissino" in 1524.

Despite being 4,300 miles long, the Amazon River doesn't have any bridges so the only way it can be crossed is boat or plane.

Earthworms don't drown as we would as they don't have lungs. They can survive several days underwater if the water is oxygenated.

Humans can only sense temperature and pressure. We do not sense wetness.

Ravens and wolves often play together.

Scientists studied data from Wisconsin and found that introducing wolves reduced the number of deer which resulted in a reduction in vehicle collisions by 24%.

Approximately 10% of the population are left handed. This more than doubles with premature babies.

Leeches are multisegmented annelid worms with 10 stomachs, 32 brains, and a few hundred teeth

The platypus doesn't have a stomach at all. Their oesophagus goes straight to their intestines.

The longest fingernails ever were 28 feet and 4.5 inches in total. American Lee Redmond started growing them in 1979 and set the record in 2008.

Mary Shelley wrote Frankenstein when she was 18 years old.

Buckingham Palace in London, England, has 775 rooms, including 78 bathrooms.

We shake hands to show we're unarmed

The hagfish defends itself by producing copious amounts of slime which clogs potential predators up.

London's black cab drivers will not take fares for trips to Great Ormond Street Children's Hospital for mothers and children.

Alfred Hitchcock's father sent the 5 year old Hitchcock to the police to be imprisoned.

There are more squid in the ocean than fish.

In 2022 Hanson's Auctions from Derby sold a 'Vampire Slaying Kit' at auction. The buyer paid £17,000.

President Ronald Reagan believed in astrology. He consulted an astrologer on the scheduling of important events.

The Sahara Desert was green from 6,000 to 9,000 years ago.

In 1956 two men were killed by a shark off Cornwall. The men had seen the shark and thrown explosives at it. The shark then carried the explosives under their boat, and they all died.

When the British monarch visits parliament she takes a Member of Parliament hostage at Buckingham Palace to ensure her safe return. It is more tradition than a strict necessity these days.

The Darvaza gas crater in Turkmenistan is a natural gas field which is burning from a crater of 69 metres diameter. It has been alight for over 50 years and is known as the Gates of Hell.

In 1929 at Princeton University Professor Glen Wever and assistant Charles Bray experimented by making a living, but sedated, cat a functioning telephone.

The Food and Drug Administration in the USA has approved the use of maggots and leeches as medical devices.

In 2009 Dorothy Fletcher had a heart attack aboard a plane flying from Manchester to Florida. When the stewardess asked the passengers for medical assistance 15 cardiologists stood up. They were on their way to a conference.

The official bird of Madison, Wisconsin, is a plastic pink flamingo.

The Walkie-Talkie skyscraper was completed in London in 2014. Unfortunately, the concave shape focused light on to the streets and caused vehicles reaching temperatures of 117C and bursting into flames. The press called it the 'Fryscraper'.

Catgut, which used to be used for tennis rackets, is usually made from sheep or goat's intestines.

Mel Brooks' handprint on the Hollywood Walk of Fame has 6 fingers.

Australian artist Lee Hadwin is unique in that he is the only person who can produce art while he is asleep and not when he is awake.

In 1161 Henry de Blois, the Bishop of Winchester, was the largest brothel owner in England. He called his prostitutes 'Winchester Geese'.

There are over 900 stone rings in the UK. Stonehenge is the most famous.

Hasbro has trademarked the smell of Play-Doh.

A 2011 study on lost remotes found that 49% of the time it was found in the couch, 8% found it in the bathroom, 8% in a dresser drawer, 4% in the fridge/freezer, and 2% percent found the remote outside.

Frogs can vomit by what is known as a 'full gastric inversion'. This is when the body doesn't just eject the vomit but also the stomach itself.

In 1999 NASA's $327m Mars Climate Orbiter crashed into the surface of Mars before it could begin operations. The cause of the failure was a mix up between metric and imperial units meant the craft was on the wrong trajectory.

Alexander Graham Bell wasn't the inventor of the telephone. He was just the first to patent it. The person who invented the telephone was Italian inventor Antonio Meucci.

NASA uses a countdown on rocket launches to build suspense. They got the idea from a 1929 Fritz Lang film.

The appearance of Halley's Comet in 1910 created some hysteria and doomsday predictions. Two enterprising Texas men were selling some anti-comet pills. They were arrested but their clients rioted till they were released.

According to the Consumer Protection Safety Commission vending machines have been responsible for at least 37 deaths and 113 injuries since 1978.

The Centre for Disease Control in the USA reports that there on average 11 drowning deaths per day in the USA. 300 of these are in the bath annually.

Snowflakes fall at approximately 1.5 mph. On average they travel for 45 minutes before hitting the ground.

The oceans are 3,700 metres (12,100 feet) deep on average.

Saffron is the most expensive spice and is derived from the crocus plant. It takes approximately 150,000 crocus' to produce 1 kg of saffron, which all have to be picked by hand.

In 1987 an 18 year old Mike Hayes funded his education at the University of Illinois by asking 2.8m people to send him a penny.

Betty Robinson won the 100m at the 1928 Amsterdam Olympics. In 1931 she was in a plane crash and initially believed to be dead. However, she survived, and she was 6 months in a wheelchair and it was 2 years before she could walk normally. Betty was part 0f the 4 x 100m relay team that won gold at the 1936 Berlin Olympics

In 2022 a hacker took down the North Korean internet. It was revealed that the hacker, known only as P4x, conducted the hack from his home in the US while watching Aliens in his pyjama pants and eating spicy corn snacks.

Ukrainians Alexandr Kudlay and Viktoria Pustovitova handcuffed themselves together on Valentine's Day 2021. This lasted for 123 days before they decided to split up.

A 7.7-hectare lot located in the quiet village of Shrewsbury, Ontario was on sale in 2022 for a real bargain price of $80,000. The blurb said 'This property is presently under water but could have endless possibilities in the future, be creative'.

In 2013, a single 487 pound Bluefin tuna sold for $1.76 million.

José Salvador Alvarenga spent 14 months adrift on the Pacific Ocean before being rescued in 2014.

Operation Flagship was a 1985 sting by the authorities. Letters were sent to fugitives last known address saying that they had won tickets to a Washington Redskins game. There were over 100 arrests.

In 2020 the longest lightning bolt was measured at 477.2 miles over Mississippi, Louisiana and Texas.

Some DVDs of "Monty Python and the Holy Grail" include a subtitle track called "Subtitles For People Who Don't Like The Film". These subtitles are from Shakespeare's Henry IV Part 2 and are vaguely like what is being said in the film.

When engineers working on the first iPod presented it to Steve Jobs, he said it was too big. The engineers said it was impossible to make it smaller. He dropped in an aquarium and pointed to the bubbles and said 'That means there is space in there. Make it smaller'.

In 1970 Jimmy Carter hired a convicted murderer, Mary Prince, as a nanny to his daughter Amy. When he was elected President she was allowed to live and work at the White House when Jimmy Carter was designated as her parole officer.

Clark's nutcracker is a North American bird that can bury and cache up to 98,000 seeds per season.

Gold can grow on trees. The Commonwealth Scientific and Industrial Research Organisation, or CSIRO, in

Kensington, Western Australia announced finding tiny grains of the precious metal in the leaves of eucalyptus trees.

Yucca moths play an important role in the survival of yucca plants. Without the yucca moth, the yucca plant would lose its only pollinator, and without the plant, the moth would lose its food source. Each depends on the other for survival.

On May 25 1935, Jesse Owens established 4 world records in athletics in 45 minutes.

There is a species of orchid (Rhizanthella gardneri) in Western Australia that spends its entire life cycle underground.

Gravity moves at the speed of light and does not act instantaneously. If the sun were to disappear for some reason the Earth would continue in its orbit for 8 minutes 20 seconds.

In England and Wales, it is legal for a 5 year old to have alcohol so long as it is on private premises.

Humpback whales catch fish in a 'bubble net'.

Japan has a conviction rate of over 99%, most of which are secured on the back of a confession.

The 1934 mystery novel Cain's Jawbone by Edward Powys Mathers is printed with its 100 pages out of order.

In 1524, a venerated statue of the Virgin Mary in the Cathedral was denounced as a witch and given a trial by water in the Dvina River. The statue floated, so it was denounced as a witch and burnt at Kubsberg.

Encephalitis lethargica is a disease which attacks the brain. From 1915 – 1926 there was a pandemic of the disease which left an estimated 500,000 dead. The pandemic mysteriously disappeared in 1927.

The Tongan castaways were a group of six Tongan teenage boys who shipwrecked on the uninhabited island of 'Ata in 1965 and lived there for 15 months until their rescue.

Owl chicks sleep on their stomachs because their heads are so big.

The largest earthworm is the Giant Gippsland earthworm found in Australia. They can measure 3 metres long.

In 2011 British intelligence service MI6 has hacked into an al-Qaeda website and added a cupcake recipe.

The first Polish language encyclopedia was published in 1745. Its definitions included "Horse: Everyone knows what a horse is", and "Goats are a stinking kind of animal".

Chess boxing is a real sport. Players alternate rounds of blitz chess and boxing. A player wins by checkmate or knockout.

Owls can rotate their heads a complete 270 degrees.

The oldest spider is an Australian trap door spider called 'Number 16'. It was studied for 43 years.

Ray Bradbury wrote the first draft of "Fahrenheit 451" on a coin-operated typewriter in the basement of the UCLA library. It charged 10¢ for 30 minutes, and he spent $9.80 in total at the machine.

China didn't win an Olympic medal till 1984.

The town of Rjukan, Norway installed 50 square meters of mirrors on a mountain so they can get some sun in the winter. The project cost $850,000.

The world record for the highest vehicle mileage on a car belongs to the late Irving Gordon and his 1966 Volvo 1800S, which has over 3,200,000 miles on it.

Bird's Nest Soup is made from the solidified spit of birds called swiftlets

In 1929 Einstein handed a courier a signed note in lieu of a tip. It had one sentence, written in German: "A calm and humble life will bring more happiness than the pursuit of success and the constant restlessness that comes with it." It sold for $1.56m at auction.

The odds of an average golfer getting a hole in one on a 200 yard par three are 150,000 to 1.

A Dyson Sphere is a hypothetical megastructure that surrounds a sun to capture all the solar energy. Some believe alien cultures may have built such structures.

The maximum height a tree can reach is around 130 metres due to the problem of transporting water to the top.

While on an African safari the author Ernest Hemmingway survived two plane crashes in two days. He was presumed dead until he was seen emerging from the jungle with a bottle of gin.

Birds can rest half their brain by keeping one eye open while asleep.

The first fire brigade was created by Marcus Licinius Crassus. He created his own brigade of 500 slaves. They rushed to burning buildings at the first cry of alarm. Upon arriving Crassus offered to buy the burning building from the distressed property owner, at a derisory price. If the owner agreed to sell the property, his men would put out the fire, if the owner refused, then they would simply let the structure burn to the ground.

After a plane crash in Pakistan in 2019 an inquiry found that 40% of pilots have 'fake licenses'. They get someone else to sit the exam for them.

In 1996 Goran Kropp travelled 8,000 miles from Stockholm to Mt Everest on a bike with 108kg of gear. He then climbed Everest without oxygen support and proceeded to cycle home.

At the centre of every snowflake is a dust particle which forms the 'seed' from which the snowflake will grow.

When Antonous Mockus, a mathematician and philosopher, became mayor of Bogotá, he hired 420 mimes to improve both traffic and citizens' behaviour. The mimes would ridicule bad drivers and pedestrians who didn't follow the rules. He believed Colombians were more afraid of ridicule than a fine.

In Tikrit, Iraq, there's a 6 ft. tall monument of the shoe that the journalist Muntadhar al-Zeidi threw at George Bush.

The word taser is an acronym for Thomas A. Swift's Electric Rifle. This is a reference to a character in a book who is the inventor of gadgets.

In the USA men and women play tennis tournaments with different tennis balls.

The longest US presidential inauguration speech was made by William Henry Harrison at 8,445 words in awful weather. Harrison died of pneumonia on April 4th, making him the shortest reigning US president ever.

In 1930, engineers rotated an 8-story, 11,000 ton Indiana Bell building a full 90 degrees. This was to allow the construction of a second building on the site. They did it while 600 employees continued working inside.

In 2004 the German Football club Union Berlin needed £1.5m to fend off bankruptcy. The supporters organised a 'bleed for Union' campaign in which they would donate blood and forward the reimbursement to the club.

The world's bestselling drug is Atorvastatin, the cholesterol drug. Between 1997 and 2011, when its patent expired, it generated $125 billion for Pfizer.

CNN has produced a Doomsday video to be played in the event of an apocalypse by the last surviving employee.

The African lungfish can live in suspended animation, called aestivation, without food and water for three to five years. They wake up when water becomes available.

From 1923 – 39 the Phoebus cartel oligopoly controlled the manufacture of incandescent light bulbs. They lowered the useful life of bulbs from 2,500 hours to 1,000 hours and increased prices to maximise profits.

In the 1700s it was believed that the sound of a bell could dispel thunder. In France, between 1753 and 1786 103 bell ringers were killed during thunderstorms.

'Newton's Flaming Laser Sword' is a philosophical razor which says that 'If a question cannot be answered through experiment, it is not worth asking'.

Leonardo da Vinci was a wedding planner between 1489 and 1493.

Abibliophobia is the fear of running out of material to read.

ONE LAST THING

If you have enjoyed this book, I would love you to write a review of it on Amazon. It is really useful feedback as well as untold encouragement to the author.

Any remarks are highly appreciated, so if you have any comments, or suggestions for improvements to this publication, or for other books, I would love to hear from you.

You can contact me at
m.prefontaine2@gmail.com

All your input is greatly valued, and the books have already been revised and improved as a result of helpful suggestions from readers.

Thank you.

Made in United States
North Haven, CT
09 April 2023

35231212R00075